Nutrition Healing

Heal the Body with Grain Free Meals and Juicing

Julia Delgado and Carol Kim

Table of Contents

CHAPTER 5: YOUR 7 DAY JUICING DIET MEAL PLAN

Introduction

The body is a marvelous functioning machine. Give it the right sustenance and it will work right and even heal itself. Give it junk and it will react much as a vehicle does when given bad gas. Eating unhealthy food gives the body a host of problems, many stemming from the excessive weight gain. We are what we eat and if we eat junk then our health will go to junk as well. Our body is remarkable though; if we feed it the right foods, it will work to correct ill health issues and will work in prevention of future health issues.

Food is nature's pharmacy. Junk food, or foods high in bad carbs (sugars and fats) are like recreational drugs, if you eat too much you will become severely addicted and your health will suffer greatly. On the other hand if you eat nutritious food it acts like good medicine, going into the body and healing all that ails it.

The body pulls the wonderful nutrients from the nutritious foods, foods such as fresh fruits and vegetables and lean proteins. These nutrients are what help to heal the body and prevent future disease. Some of the greatest benefits from eating right aside from healing from illnesses are weight management and a stronger immune system.

Weight Issues

Just being overweight causes many health issues in the body including high blood pressure, joint and muscle pain, high cholesterol, and high blood sugar. These reasons alone should prompt people to want to lose weight. Often if the weight is lost, the health issues will go away or at least will be more manageable. There are many different diets out there to help lose weight. Some are so complicated that people give up too fast. The success of a diet plan comes first with the mental attitude toward it and secondly with the idea that the diet starts a lifestyle change.

You can go on a diet, lose the weight and then you may think you can go back to your old ways of eating. This will only disappoint you because if you go back to your old eating habits the weight will come back, guaranteed. In order to maintain weight loss you must change your eating habits, permanently. The diet plans listed here, the grain free and juicing diet are both excellent nutritious diets to help with weight loss. In order to be successful with these two diets you must break the food addiction first.

Breaking the Food Addiction

With junk food being highly addictive people often have a very tough time starting and sticking with new diets. This is because the craving for the junk food out-weighs the desire for the diet. This is the number one reason for diet failure. You can do something to help this not be an issue, even if you have a severe food addiction. You can wean from the junk food before the start the new diet, or you can wean from the junk food as you start the new diet.

It takes the human body a good three weeks, or twenty-one days to develop a good habit and also to break a bad habit. You should give yourself three weeks to break the junk food addiction if you have one before you dive into the new diet plans. If you don't take the time to do this you will likely cheat or quit the diet and then you will not be any better for it.

Some may ask if they can just stop the junk food all at once. While the answer is yes, of course, there are some undesirable side effects. A junk food addiction is as real as an addiction to cigarettes or alcohol. If you deprive your body of it your body will go into a very real and very intense craving for it. You will feel hungry and nothing will satisfy the urge. You may experience headaches and moodiness too. You can avoid this if you properly wean from the junk food.

You may need to keep a food journal for a week, which will add a week to your weaning process, or if you have a good memory, think back and write down all the food you have eaten over the past week. Record every snack, every morsel you eat. Record the time you eat, how much, and what. This will give you a great indication of what you're up against in busting the junk food addiction.

Next, take the amount of junk food you eat on a daily basis and divide it up over a three week time. You will want to start slow. The first few days replace one instance of junk food with a healthy food. Maybe try a grain free or juicing recipe from this book. Give yourself a few days to become accustomed to the new food.

Once you start the weaning, remove a junk food instance every few days replacing it with nutritious foods. Give your body a few days between each time you take the junk food away. This way your body will wean slowly at the bad side-effects will not be an issue or will at the very least be manageable. By the end of the three weeks, you will have successfully weaned from the junk food. The hope is that you will not crave it any longer or feel any moodiness, cravings, or headaches. You may crave it once in a while, but you can just choose to eat a healthier snack and stick on the diet. This makes your dieting a lifestyle change rather than a temporary fix to lose weight (or lower blood pressure, cholesterol, etc.)

Disclaimer

This book is for informational purposes only. This book is not meant to diagnose, treat, or offer promises. If you have health concerns, you should seek the advice of a health care provider. You should always discuss any new diet change and your health concerns with them before starting a new diet.

Section 1: Grain Free Recipes

There's something absolutely delicious about a freshly baked loaf of bread, a crispy waffle, or a tasty cake hot out of the oven! These foods all have one thing in common: they're made with grain or wheat flour. Cooking with wheat flour and grain is something that everyone does, and it produces a whole lot of delicious foods.

Unfortunately for many, grain and wheat are things that they cannot enjoy. Gluten intolerance can be a serious problem for many people, and they are unable to eat foods that contain lots of grain or wheat. When they do, they have serious digestive problems, or their body can react strongly and negatively to the gluten in the grain that they are eating.

Gluten has been linked to a number of problems. Interestingly enough, the body often sees gluten as being a foreign substance that it can't process. While gluten is commonly found in the food we eat, it wasn't always part of our diet. The human body can't always process this gooey, sticky protein easily, and it can be a bit hard on the body if you happen to be sensitive to it. Even those without celiac problems may not be able to handle the gluten, as their bodies react to the "foreign substance" by attacking it with antibodies.

Cutting grain out of your diet can help to reduce your risk of health problems, especially if you have celiac disorder or other gluten-sensitive problems. However, even for those that don't have these health problems, it may be a good idea to cut gluten out of your diet. Many people don't have celiac disease, and yet they still experience the drawbacks of eating gluten.

In an article in the New Zealand edition of Stuff magazine, an article by a world-renowned expert on food allergies, Dr. Rodney Ford, states, "Gluten causes tiredness, anxiety and stress. The medical world accepts it can damage the gut, but it can also damage the brain, skin and nerves. Until now, many of these illnesses have been blamed on everything from stress at home to other medical conditions, including depression." [1]

Cutting gluten out of your life isn't just something you can do to prevent celiac problems, but it can be good for your health. Many holistic doctors and therapists will recommend cutting it from your diet, as it carries the risk of causing negative side effects.

Did you know that eliminating grain and gluten can be beneficial to your body? The benefits include:

- Reduced risk of IBS or other digestive problems
- Less chance of becoming fatigued, depressed, nauseous, or developing stomach cramps
- Boost in your energy levels
- Reduced body fat percentage
- Increase in lean muscle tissue
- Lowered blood pressure
- Improved mood and sense of wellbeing
- As you can see, there are many great reasons to cut grain from your diet!

"But," you may say, "all of my favorite foods are made with grain! How can I cut grain out of my diet and still enjoy the food I'm eating?"

Don't worry about it! In this book, you'll find plenty of delicious recipes that you can make without needing to use grain, and you can whip up your favorite dishes and still make them gluten-free. You'll have to spend a bit of money to stock your house with some ingredients you probably don't have right now, but you'll be amazed at how many delicious foods you can make without using grain.

Enjoy the book, and happy grain-free cooking!

Tasty Grain Free Recipes

Grain Free Breaded Chicken

There's nothing like some breaded chicken to kick off your lunch in style, but bread crumbs have wheat, right? Here is a quick and easy recipe you can use to make breaded chicken without the bread...

Ingredients

For this dish, you will need:

1 large chicken breast
1 cup of almond flour
½ cup of Kraft's Parmesan Cheese
Thyme
Basil
Oregano
½ cup of butter
Red or crushed chili pepper
Garlic powder
Salt and pepper, to taste

Preparation:

To begin, slice the chicken breast into steaks -- preferably about three steaks from each half of the breast. You should have about 6 medium steaks from the breast.

Preheat your oven to about 350 F. Use a bit of butter to grease the bottom of a baking tray.

In a bowl, combine the almond flour with the Parmesan cheese. Sprinkle in about a teaspoon each of basil, thyme, and oregano, and add in a pinch of crushed red pepper for some spice. A teaspoon of garlic powder will help to add the flavor you want, and a bit of salt and black pepper will round out the flavors.

In a saucepan, melt the butter. Dip the chicken steaks into the butter, ensuring that the entire surface of the chicken is coated well. Roll the buttered strips in the almond flour, and make sure that they are properly coated with the flour mixture.

Place the steaks onto your baking tray, laying them as flat as possible. Transfer the tray into the oven, and let the steaks cook for about 20 minutes. They should be a wonderful golden brown, and they will be absolutely delightful to eat! (Check to make sure that they aren't pink in the center, as that's a sign that the chicken is undercooked.)

Sesame Seed Chicken Fried Steak

Want to eat that Southern-style chicken fried steak that your mama used to make you? This simple recipe won't make it exactly like the regular steak, but it's as close as you'll get while on a gluten-free diet!

Ingredients

For this dish, you will need:
4 large steaks, sliced fairly thin
2 eggs
½ cup of almond flour
1/3 cup of sesame seeds
1/4 cup of flax seeds
Chicken bouillon powder
Basil
Bay leaves
Garlic powder
Salt and black pepper, to taste

Preparation:

To begin, place a pan on the stove to heat, and add in enough oil to deep fry your breaded steak. Let the oil heat as you go about preparing the rest of the meal.

Crack the 2 eggs into a bowl, and beat them vigorously to combine the egg and yolk. Add a pinch of salt into the eggs.

Combine the almond flour, a pinch each of chicken bouillon, garlic powder, salt, and pepper, and the flax seeds in a bowl. Add the sesame seeds into the bowl, and crush three bay leaves in your hands to add them into the mix. Use a fork to stir the dry ingredients together, and make sure that they're properly combined before moving on.

Dip each steak into the eggs, and roll the dipped meat into the flour and seed mixture. Make sure that the entire surface of the meat has been properly coated. If you want to really get the flour coating on right, you can roll the meat in the flour before dipping it into the egg, and roll it a second time after dipping to ensure that the layer of flour is very thick.

Place the steaks in the hot oil one at a time, and cook them until they are golden brown. Remove them from the pan once they are properly cooked, and place them on a plate with paper towels beneath and above them to soak up the oil.

Let the steaks sit until they are all cooked, transfer onto

a plate, and serve.

Gluten and Sugar-Free Gingerbread Cake

Want a delicious dessert to make your Christmas celebrations complete? This gluten and sugar-free gingerbread cake will have all of the flavor of the holiday, but with none of the unhealthy nutrients that you're trying to avoid!

Ingredients:

For this cake, you will need:
½ cup of coconut flour
1 cup of amaranth flour
1 cup of buckwheat flour
2 tablespoons of flax meal (For those who want the non-vegan version of this cake, use 2 eggs instead of the flax meal. It will make the cake a bit fluffier, and will help to round out the flavors nicely.)
2 ½ teaspoons of baking soda
Ground cinnamon
Ground ginger
Ground cloves
Ground nutmeg
Salt
Water
¾ cup of agave nectar
¾ cup of molasses

Canola oil

Fresh ginger

Lemon zest

Preparation:

To begin, turn on the oven and let it heat to 350 F. As the oven is heating, prepare the cake.

Combine the coconut flour, amaranth flour, buckwheat flour, and baking soda in a bowl. Add in 2 teaspoons of cinnamon, the same amount of ground ginger, half a teaspoon each of cloves, salt, and nutmeg, and a teaspoon or two of lemon zest. Stir the ingredients well to combine.

In a separate bowl, combine the flax meal with a few tablespoons of water, and stir in the agave, the molasses, ¾ of a cup of canola oil, and a couple of teaspoons of the grated fresh ginger. Mix these ingredients together well, and pour them into the bowl with the dry ingredients. Stir the wet and dry ingredients together to make the batter for the cake, and add about a cup of boiling water to your final batter.

Once the water has been properly mixed in with the rest of the ingredients, pour the cake batter into a buttered baking pan. Place the pan into the oven, and let it cook for about 40 minutes.

You'll find that a toothpick or knife inserted into the center of the cake will come out clean, and it will let you know that your cake is ready to enjoy.

Cut once the cake has cooled a bit, and serve.

Gluten Free Waffles

There's nothing like a heaping stack of waffles to get your morning started the right way, but your regular waffles are loaded with grain and gluten. These delicious grain-free waffles will be the perfect breakfast, and it will help you to enjoy what you're eating without having to worry about adding grain to your diet.

Ingredients

For this dish, you will need:

1 cup of rice flour

1/3 cups of potato starch (not all cornstarch products are gluten-free)

3 tablespoons of tapioca flour

1 ½ teaspoons of baking powder

½ teaspoon of baking soda

Salt

Xanthan gum

Buttermilk

Sugar substitute

2 eggs

Canola oil

2 cups of water

Preparation:

To begin, heat your waffle iron. It takes about 5 to 10 minutes for the waffle iron to heat -- depending on the brand -- so make sure that it's heating as you go about preparing the waffles.

Mix the rice flour, potato starch, tapioca flour, baking soda, and baking powder together in a bowl. Add in about half a teaspoon of salt, and the same amount of xanthan gum. Mix the dry ingredients together, and be sure that they are properly combined before moving on to the next step.

Crack the two eggs into another bowl, and add in the water. Add about 3 tablespoons of the oil, and mix the ingredients together well. Stir them in with the dry ingredients, and mix until you get the waffle batter you want. The batter will be a bit thick, so add buttermilk to produce the desired consistency for the waffle batter. Make sure that there are no lumps.

Use some spray cooking oil to grease the waffle iron, or use regular oil on a paper towel to cover the iron with a thin layer of oil. Pour the batter into the heated iron, and close the lid. Watch the waffle iron until the light turns off, and use a fork to remove the cooked waffle from the waffle maker.

Serve while hot, and enjoy the delicious, crunchy
waffles!

Buckwheat Pancakes

For those of you who just can't stay away from those flapjacks, this pancake recipe will be the perfect grain-free solution for you! You'll still be able to have a tall stack of delicious pancakes, but without worrying about gluten or grain.

Ingredients

For this dish, you will need:
1 ½ cups of buckwheat flour
3 tablespoons of sugar (use sugar alternative for a low-sugar meal)
Salt
1 teaspoon of baking soda
Unsalted butter
1 egg
Buttermilk

Preparation:

To begin, place a frying pan on the stove to heat. Make sure that it has been properly heated before placing the batter onto the pan, so give it time to warm up as you make the pancakes.

Mix the flour, sugar, and baking soda together in a bowl. Add in about a teaspoon of salt. Stir the ingredients well to combine.

Crack your egg in another bowl, and beat to combine the yolk and white.

Melt the butter in a saucepan or the microwave, and pour the melted butter over the flour mixture -- stirring as you pour. Add the egg into the mix, and pour in about a cup of buttermilk as well. Stir the batter together, and you'll have a fairly thick mixture. Keep pouring in buttermilk until your pancakes have reached the desired consistency, and stir to ensure that there are no lumps.

Once the batter has been prepared, pour it into a pitcher or an empty ketchup bottle. Gently pour or squeeze the batter onto your heated pan, which you will have coated with a bit of oil to butter to prevent the pancakes from sticking.

Cook until the top of the pancake is riddled with bubbles, and flip it over to cook on the other side for about 20 seconds.

Once the batter has been used up, you'll have a delicious stack of healthy buckwheat pancakes that are grain-free and fairly low calorie!

Grain-Free Cornbread

You can't have chili beans without some delicious cornbread, and there are so many other dishes that won't be complete without this delicious savory baked bread. Don't worry about it being high in grain, as we've substituted the ingredients in the bread for grain-free ones!

Ingredients

For this dish, you will need:
1 ½ cups of cornmeal
1 cup of millet flour
1 cup of rice flour
2 eggs
Water
Vegetable oil
¼ cup of sugar
1 tablespoon of baking powder
Salt

Preparation:

To begin, heat your oven to about 400 degrees. This way, it will be hot enough to cook the bread, but it won't be so hot that the bread will burn.

Use a bit of butter to grease a 9x9 baking dish, and set it aside as you prepare the bread.

In a bowl, crack and beat the eggs vigorously to combine the yolk and egg white. Heat 1 ½ cups of water until they are lukewarm, and add them into the eggs. Drop in ¼ cup of canola or vegetable oil, and mix the ingredients well until they are properly blended.

In a separate bowl, mix the millet flour, rice flour, and cornmeal together. Add in the white sugar, the baking powder, and about a teaspoon of salt. Make sure that the dry ingredients are all mixed together properly, and hollow out a hole in the center of the bowl.

Pour the wet ingredients into the hollowed center of the flour mixture, and use a whisk to stir the ingredients together properly. Whisk and stir until you are sure that there are no lumps, which could take a few minutes.

Once you're sure there are no lumps, pour the batter into the greased baking pan. Place the pan into the oven, and let it cook for about 20 minutes. You can tell that it's cooked by pressing on the surface of the bread. If it's properly done, the corn bread will spring back up when you press gently on it.

Remove from the oven, let the cornbread cool for a few minutes, and serve while still warm.

Curried Quinoa

This delicious side dish is made without any grain, which means that you can eat it whenever you want! The quinoa is a much lower-calorie alternative to rice, but it will be a delicious alternative that will make the dish absolutely fantastic!

Ingredients:

For this dish, you will need:
1 cup of quinoa
Olive oil
1 onion
Garlic
2 cups of chicken broth
Curry powder
Ancho chili powder
Salt and pepper

Preparation:

To begin, place a skillet on the stove to heat. Bring it to medium heat, and pour a couple of tablespoons of olive oil into the pan.

Chop the onion very finely, and add between 3 and 5

cloves of garlic -- depending on your flavor preference. Cook the aromatics in the oil, leaving them in the pan for about 5 minutes to ensure that you have extracted the flavor from them. Add the quinoa into the pan, and cook the seed in the oil until it is lightly toasted.

Once you're done cooking the quinoa, pour the chicken broth into the pan. Cover the pan, and let the broth heat until it begins to boil. Stir in about a tablespoon each of the curry powder and Mexican chili powder, and cover the pan once again.

Turn the heat down to let the quinoa simmer, and let it cook on low heat for about 25 minutes. The quinoa should be soft and tasty, and you can add a bit of salt and pepper to add the flavor you want for the dish. (Serve as the starch with nearly any protein, and it will be a delicious companion for your meal!)

Roasted Almond Cookies

Want to enjoy a delicious dessert without getting into the grain-loaded cookie jar? These cookies are quick and easy to make, and you'll find that they're the perfect grain-free solution to help you stay true to your gluten-free diet!

Ingredients:

For this dish, you will need:
1 cup of raw almonds
½ cup of maple syrup
1 cup of oat flour
Almond extract

Preparation:

Preheat the oven to about 275 F, which will be hot enough to toast the almonds.

Place the cup of almonds onto a baking sheet, and put them in the oven. Let them heat until they become golden brown and are releasing a delightful scent, which will take about 40 minutes. Be careful that they don't burn.

Once the almonds are cooked, remove them from the oven and set them aside to cool. After they have cooled down enough, run them through your food processor to produce a fine almond flour.

Mix the flour in a bowl together with the oat flour, maple syrup, and almond extract.

Turn the heat of the oven up to 350 F, and let it heat.

As the oven is heating, use your hands to form the dough into 6 balls. Press the balls gently to flatten them a bit, until they are about half an inch thick. Place the cookies onto a greased baking sheet, and put the sheet in the oven.

Let the cookies bake for about 12 minutes, but keep a close eye on them because the edges can burn very quickly. They will become browned and crisp around the edges of the cookie, and that's how you'll know that they're done.

Remove them from the oven, let them cool, and enjoy!

Grain-Free Zucchini Bread

Most people think of banana bread or carrot cake as being the only vegetable-laden desserts that you can make, but you'll find that zucchini bread will be a delicious alternative that will be just as healthy and tasty! Thanks to the grain-free recipe, you won't have to worry about the gluten.

Ingredients:

For this dish, you will need:
1 cup of teff flour
1 cup of buckwheat flour
Baking soda
Salt
Baking powder
3 eggs
Lemon zest
Cinnamon
1 cup of apple sauce
½ cup of maple syrup
Coconut oil
Vanilla extract
2 cups of grated zucchini
1 cup of raisins and almonds mixed

Preparation:

To begin, turn on your oven and pre-heat it to about 350 degrees. As it's heating, move on to the next step.

Mix the buckwheat and teff flours together in a bowl, and add in a tablespoon of cinnamon, a teaspoon of salt and lemon zest each, 2 teaspoons of the baking soda, and ¼ teaspoon of baking powder. Stir well to ensure that the ingredients are properly combined before moving on.

In a separate bowl, combine the apple sauce and maple syrup together, and crack the three eggs into the bowl. Beat well to mix the ingredients, and add two teaspoons of vanilla extract and a tablespoon of coconut oil into the bowl. Stir well to mix.

Once the wet ingredients are properly mixed, pour the dry ingredients into the bowl. Stir well or use an electric mixer to combine the ingredients, and stir until there are no more lumps. Pour the zucchini into the batter, and add the raisins and almonds as well. Mix to distribute these ingredients.

Pour the batter into a greased baking pan, which should have a bit of butter along the bottom to help make the cake tasty. Put the pan into the oven, and let it cook for about 50 minutes. The cake will take longer to cook than your average flour cake, but you'll know that it's done when a toothpick or knife inserted into the center of the cake comes out clean.

Remove the cake from the oven, let cool for a few minutes, cut, and serve!

Apple Cobbler

Not quite the same as Apple Crumble, this Apple Cobbler recipe is the perfect grain-free breakfast treat! It will be crunchy, flavorful, and delightful, but it won't have any of the gluten that you're trying so hard to avoid.

Ingredients

For this dish, you will need:
6 apples
1 can of cranberry sauce
Brown sugar
1 cup of steel-cut oats
Cinnamon
Soy milk
Butter

Preparation:

To begin, peel and cut the apples. You will want to make them small slices, easy enough to fit into your mouth without being too small.

Preheat the oven to about 350 F once the apples are done. Grease a baking tray with a bit of butter, and set it aside as you move on.

Combine the apples and the cranberry sauce in a bowl, and add in 2 or 3 tablespoons of the brown sugar. Add ¼ cup of soy milk, and mix the ingredients well to ensure that they are properly combined.

Melt a bit of butter on the stove, and pour the butter over the top of the oats. Toss the oats to coat them evenly with the butter.

Place the apple mixture into the pan, and cover it with a top layer of oats. Place the pan into the oven, and let it cook for about 35 or 40 minutes. You'll see that the oats turn a pleasant golden brown, and the juices released by the apple and cranberry sauce will bubble nicely.

Remove from the oven, let cool for a few minutes, and serve as the perfect healthy breakfast!

Breakfast Cereal Sans Gluten

A healthy breakfast cereal can be the perfect thing to get your morning started the right way, as it will provide you with slow-burning carbs that will give you energy all day long. This breakfast cereal will be perfect, as it comes without grain and will give you that energy boost you need for the long day ahead.

Ingredients:

For this dish, you will need:
½ cup of quinoa
½ cup of buckwheat groats
1 cup of brown basmati rice
½ cup of millet
½ cup of flax seeds
½ cup of sesame seeds
½ cup of cornmeal
½ cup of amaranth

Preparation:

To begin, place the basmati rice into a blender or grinder, and grind until you have produced a coarse rice flour. Empty the rice into a bowl.

Grind or blend all of the other ingredients, and you will end up with a mixture of various flours -- none of which will be wheat or grain flour, of course.

To prepare the cereal, put 4 cups of water into a pan to boil on the stove. Once the water is boiling, add in about a cup of the cereal mixture and a pinch of salt. Add a tablespoon or two of milk powder, and let the ingredients cook until they have thickened.

To add some flavor, add in a bit of cinnamon, some butter, and a tablespoon of sugar. You'll find that these ingredients will sweeten the cereal, and a bit of milk will help to make it more edible.

The cereal mixture will take about 20 minutes to cook, and you should keep the heat low to prevent it from burning. After 20 minutes has passed, scoop into a bowl, let cool for a minute, and enjoy!

Rice Stuffing

Need to stuff that Thanksgiving turkey but don't want to use bread? This rice turkey or chicken stuffing will be the perfect thing for you! It's tasty, subtle, and easy to make, and it will enable you to give your turkey the right filling.

Ingredients:

For this dish, you will need:
2 cups of white rice
Water
Chicken bouillon
1 onion
Butter
Garlic
1 celery stalk
Parsley
Salt
Sage
Thyme
Pepper, to taste

Preparation:

To begin, you will need to dice the onions as fine as you

can. Make sure to chop the onions very small.

Place a pot on the stove to heat, and add about a tablespoon of butter into the bottom of the pan. Once the butter has melted, add the onions into the mixture. Let the onions fry for a minute, and chop the garlic as you do so. Add about 5 cloves of garlic -- chopped fine -- into the pan, and fry the garlic along with the onions.

Once the onions have begun to brown around the edges, add the uncooked rice into the pan. You will want to cook the rice until it shows signs of beginning to burn, and the grains will become slightly browned. At this point, add the 2 cups of water into the pan, and cover it.

Once the rice begins to simmer, add a tablespoon or two of chicken bouillon into the pan. Dice the celery stalk, and drop the pieces into the pan. Sprinkle parsley, salt, sage, thyme, and all the pepper you want into the rice.

The simmering water will cook the rice in about 20 minutes, but keep a close eye on it. once the level of the rice rises above the water level, you only have about 5 to 7 more minutes until the rice is completely cooked. Make sure the rice doesn't burn, and don't let it cook all the way. The rice should still be a bit crunchy when you turn it off.

Once the rice is cooked, remove it from the pan, let it cool, and use it to stuff your turkey. The partially cooked rice will finish cooking as the turkey cooks, and it will come out soft and fluffy!

Gluten Free Irish Shortbread

There's nothing like a good piece of Irish shortbread to eat after your Irish beef stew, and you'll find that a hearty piece of this bread will go down nicely. The best part about this bread: it's made without gluten or wheat!

Ingredients

For this dish, you will need:
2 cups of butter
2 cups of rye flour
1 cup of corn flour
2 cups of brown sugar

Preparation:

To begin, heat the oven to 300 degrees. Take the time to grease two baking pans, or use grease paper to prevent a mess.

Soften the butter in a double boiler, or leave it at room temperature for an hour to make it easier to mash. Use a fork to mix the sugar into the butter, and combine it until it is creamy and blended. Add the corn flour and the rye flour, and combine into a nice dough.

Divide the dough that you have into two portions, and press each portion of dough into the pans that you have prepared. Use the fork to prick some shallow holes, dividing the bread into individual portions. You can sprinkle a bit of sugar to make it decorative.

Place the baking pans into the oven, and let them cook for about an hour. You'll find that the bread can cook in as little time as 45 minutes, so keep an eye on it. You may notice that the edges of the bread are getting browned, and the top will be nicely golden.

Cut the bread into individual pieces while it is still warm, and enjoy!

Asian Sesame Noodles

If you love the taste of the Orient, this will definitely be the dish for you. These tasty noodles are grain-free, but they're absolutely delightful! With the right ingredients added to this dish, you'll have everything you need to get your Oriental on!

Ingredients

For this dish, you will need:
400 grams of Gluten-free noodles
Sesame oil
2 carrots
Garlic
Fresh ginger root
1 onion
½ head of cabbage
½ pepper
1 sprig of cilantro
Almond butter
Gluten-free soy sauce

Preparation:

To begin, you'll need to put a pot of water on the stove to boil. Add about 3 cups of water per 100 grams of noodles, and give it a few minutes to boil.

As the water is heating up, dice the ginger, garlic, and onions. You can use as much garlic as you want, but add no more than a teaspoon of fresh ginger root. Julienne the carrots, the bell pepper, and the cabbage, making the slices as thin as possible.

Place a wok on the stove to heat, and pour in a few tablespoons of sesame oil. Once the oil is hot, drop in the ginger, garlic, and onions. Stir fry the ingredients for a few minutes, and add in the carrots. Once the carrots have begun to soften, add in the peppers and the cabbage. Cook for just 3 minutes, and add the soy sauce into the mixture.

Place the noodles in the water to cook, and keep a close eye on them. You don't want them to overcook, as they'll be quite unpleasant. Make sure that they're al dente, and remove them from the stove. Drain the water, run cold water over the noodles, and throw the noodles into the wok.

Stir fry the noodles with the other ingredients, adding a tablespoon of almond butter, 2 tablespoons of soy sauce, and ½ tablespoon of sesame oil to flavor the noodles. Cook until the liquid has all been eliminated

from the wok, leaving you with a dry, slightly fried
noodle dish.

Serve the noodles onto two plates, chop the cilantro to
sprinkle on top of the noodles, and serve with chopsticks
and your favorite Chinese hot sauce.

Shrimp Cakes

Want to enjoy some seafood, but can't eat gluten? These gluten-free shrimp cakes are an absolute delight, and they'll help you to get a lot more protein in your diet. They're fairly easy to make, but they're definitely a delicious meal that will be ideal for anyone on a weight loss diet.

Ingredients

For this dish, you will need:
1 pound of shrimp
1 red bell pepper
2 cloves of garlic
Scallions
Lime juice
Sea salt
Chipotle
1 egg
½ cup of almond flour
Grapeseed or peanut
½ cup of chopped cilantro

Preparation:

To begin, peel and de-vein the shrimp. This can be a

lengthy process, so be prepared to spend at least 20 minutes in this activity.

Once the shrimp has been prepared, throw them into the blender or food processor. Press the pulse button until the shrimp has been chopped fine, and remove the shrimp from the blender.

Pour the shrimp into a bowl, and add a teaspoon of sea salt, the cilantro, and ¼ teaspoon of chipotle. Crack the egg into the bowl, and mix it well to combine.

Dice the scallions, the garlic, and the bell pepper, making sure that they are very finely chopped. Add them into the bowl, and stir to mix properly. Add the lime juice for the finishing flavor touches.

Use your hands to form the ingredients into balls, which you will dip into the almond flour to coat them thoroughly as you flatten them into patties.

Place a skillet on the stove to heat, and add enough oil to fry the patties. Place four of the patties into the skillet at a time, and cook for about 5 minutes. Turn the patty onto its other side, and cook it until that side is also browned.

Remove the cooked patties from the pan, and place them on a paper towel to drain as you cook the rest. You should obtain about 12 patties from this mixture.

Enjoy with a simple marinara sauce, or just pour some of your favorite hot sauce over the patties to make them taste delicious!

Stuffed Bell Peppers

This dish is made with a rice stuffing that will be absolutely divine, not to mention free of gluten. If you want to enjoy a delicious stuffed bell pepper, this is a recipe that you must try!

Ingredients:

For this dish, you will need:
6 green bell peppers
Diced green chilies
1 pound of ground beef
1 onion
5 cloves of garlic
1 cup of rice
Cumin
Cilantro
Chili powder
Sea salt

Preparation:

To begin, place a pan on the stove to heat. Pour a tablespoon of oil into the bottom of the pan, and dice one of the cloves of garlic. Cook the garlic until it's nicely browned, and add the rice into the pan. Once the rice is toasted, pour 1 cup of water into the pan. Cover it and cook on low heat until the rice is done. Remove from the heat and set aside.

Dice the onion and the rest of the garlic very finely, and place a skillet on the stove to heat. With a bit of oil in the bottom of the pan, sauté the garlic and onions for a few minutes. Add the ground beef into the pan, and cook it until it's well done. Add ½ can of diced green chilies 3 minutes before the meat is done, and cook them with the meat. Once you have turned off the meat, add in a teaspoon of cumin, ½ cup of diced fresh cilantro, a teaspoon of chili powder, and a tablespoon of sea salt.

Take the ground beef mixture and add it into the pan with the rice. Mix well to combine, and add salt and pepper as desired.

Use a knife to score around the top of the bell pepper, and pull off the top to extract the seeds. Wash the peppers thoroughly to remove any remaining seeds.

Heat the oven to 350 F.

Use a spoon to scoop the rice and beef mixture into the bell peppers, stuffing them completely full. Remove the seeds from the tops of the bell peppers, and place the tops back on the peppers. Place the bell peppers on a tray, and place the tray in the oven.

Let the peppers cook for about 45 minutes to an hour, and they will be ready to eat!

Gluten-Free Turkey Club

This is a delicious sandwich that you can make all on your own, and you'll be able to use gluten-free bread to slap together this quick and easy meal. You can used gluten-free bread that you bought from the store, or you can make your own loaf of gluten-free nut bread. This recipe will just tell you how to make the perfect sandwich, but there's a recipe further down that will tell you how to make the bread.

Ingredients

For this dish, you will need:
3 slices of gluten-free bread
4 slices of turkey ham
1 avocado
2 slices of your favorite cheese
Onion
Tomato
Canned chipotle chili peppers
Lettuce
Pickles
Alfalfa sprouts
Dijon mustard
Tabasco sauce
Light mayonnaise

Preparation:

To begin, place a skillet on the stove to heat. Once the skillet is properly hot, place the bread on the skillet. Only toast one side of two slices of bread, but toast the third slice on both sides.

Remove the bread from the skillet, and start with one of the half-toasted slices placed toasted side down.

Onto this slice of bread, spread a bit of mayonnaise. Add 2 slices of turkey, one slice of cheese, 1 onion ring, two pickles, and the alfalfa sprouts. Sprinkle Tabasco sauce generously. Grab the fully toasted slice of bread, and spread Dijon mustard on one side and mayo on the other. Place the toast mustard side down on top of the other ingredients.

Add the last two slices of turkey onto the sandwich, along with the cheese, 1 slice of tomato, 1 diced canned chipotle pepper, 3 slices of avocado, and two leaves of lettuce. Sprinkle Tabasco sauce generously onto the sandwich, and spread Dijon mustard onto the untoasted side of the final piece of bread before completing your sandwich.

Cut in half, serve, and enjoy!

All Purpose, Gluten and Grain-Free Nut Bread

This is the nut bread that you can use to make sandwiches, cheese toast, eat with your morning coffee, or just snack on when you're hungry. It's a gluten and grain-free bread that you can use for just about anything, and it will be the perfect option regardless of what sweet or savory dish you need bread for. It's also quick and easy to make!

Ingredients:

For this dish, you will need:
¼ cup of flax meal
1 ½ cups of almond flour
Salt
4 eggs
½ teaspoon of baking soda
1 cup of walnuts, hazelnuts, almonds, and other nuts.
¼ cup of sesame seeds
¼ cup of amaranth
¼ cup of sunflower seeds
1 teaspoon of apple cider vinegar
1 teaspoon of agave honey

Preparation:

To begin, heat the oven to about 350 F, and grease two bread pans.

Combine the almond flour with the flax meal, baking soda, and a pinch of salt in a bowl, stirring well to ensure that the ingredients are properly combined.

Crack the eggs into a bowl, and use a fork or whisk to beat them well. Make sure they are frothy, and add into the bowl the agave honey and vinegar. Mix the wet and dry ingredients together in a bowl, and add the various nuts and seeds into the same bowl. Use a fork or whisk to mix the ingredients properly until there are no lumps.

Pour the bread batter into the greased bread pans, and put them in the oven. The bread will probably take about 30 to 40 minutes to cook, so keep an eye on them. Check the bread for doneness by inserting a knife into the center, and it will come out clean when it's done cooking.

Remove from the oven, set aside to cool, and slice the bread once it has reached room temperature. You now have the ideal loaf of bread for just about anything!

Pad Thai

Pad Thai is one of the most popular Thai dishes in the country, and it will be a wonderful grain-free alternative to the more popular Chinese and Japanese fried noodle dishes. It's fairly easy to make, and it's absolutely delicious!

Ingredients

For this dish, you will need:
6 ounces of rice noodles
Sesame oil
1 onion
1 head of broccoli
Water
4 cloves of garlic
Scallions
Cilantro
Peanuts
Salt and pepper, to taste

Preparation:

To begin, place a pot of water on the stove to boil. Bring the water to a boil, and drop the rice noodles in to cook. The package will usually have clear instructions on how to cook the noodles, so follow them precisely for al dente noodles. Drain the noodles, run cold water over them, and set them aside.

Place a skillet on the stove to heat, and add a bit of sesame oil into the bottom. Dice the onion very fine, and add it into the pan to be sautéed. Cook the onions on medium-low heat, and make sure they are nicely browned.

As the onions are cooking, cut the broccoli into bite-sized spears. Once about 10 minutes has passed, add the broccoli in with the browned onions. Add ¼ cup of water, and cover the pan. Let the broccoli sauté with the onions for roughly 5 minutes, after which time it will become soft and turn a bright color.

Add salt to the pan, and dice the garlic to be added as well. Add a bit more sesame oil to ensure that the ingredients don't dry out, and add some diced peanuts into the pan. Use a tablespoon of arrowroot powder and water to thicken the mixture, and stir fry the ingredients to ensure that the powder is spread all around.

Place the noodles onto a plate, and pour the vegetable mixture over the top. If you want to add some protein, throw some shrimp into a pan and grill them to serve on top of the vegetables and noodles.

Garnish with some scallions and diced cilantro, and enjoy!

Gluten-Free Chicken Noodle Soup

There's nothing like a cup of chicken noodle soup when you're feeling ill, but wheat noodles would just make the problem worse. With this grain-free chicken noodle soup, you'll always feel better, and it is a tasty soup that you can't help but love!

Ingredients:

For this dish, you will need:
1 liter of chicken broth
1 stalk of celery
1 onions
3 cloves of garlic
1 carrot
1 zucchini
1 pack of gluten-free noodles
½ chicken breast

Preparation:

To begin, dice the onions and the carrots very finely. Make sure that they are diced very small.

Place a pot on the stove to heat, and drop a tablespoon of olive oil into the bottom. Add the garlic and onions into the pot, and sauté them until they are browned.

Once the onions and garlic are properly cooked, add the chicken broth into the pot. Set the heat on medium, and let the broth boil.

As the broth is heating up, cut the carrots into small pieces about as large as your fingernails. Throw them into the pot, along with the celery - which you will slice into small pieces as well.

Run the zucchini through a julienne slicer, and you'll have what looks like simple noodles. Put them into the pot, and let them cook along with the other ingredients.

On the side, add a bit of butter into a skillet. Slice the chicken breast into small chunks, and cook the chicken in the pot until browned on the outside. Add the partially cooked chicken into the pot of soup, ensuring that you get all the liquid and oil from the skillet.

Turn the soup up to high heat, and let it cook for another 15 minutes. Once that time has passed, drop the gluten-free soup noodles into the mixture, and let them cook on low heat. Once the noodles have cooked properly, turn off the fire and remove the pot from the stove.

Serve, add a splash of lime, and enjoy!

Gluten-Free Potato Beef Stew

Want to make a thick, hearty stew without adding flour or wheat to the mixture? This delicious stew will be an ideal meal to have on a cold winter evening, and it will be just as rich and hearty as any stew made with flour to thicken it!

Ingredients:

For this dish, you will need:
4 potatoes
1 pound of stew meat
2 carrots
1 onion
5 cloves of garlic
½ cup of table wine
¼ cup of soy sauce
1 cup of milk
2 liters of beef broth
Salt and pepper, to taste
Preparations:

To begin, peel one potato, dice it, and place it in a small pot of water to boil. Let the potato cook for about an hour, adding more water into the pot whenever necessary. Once the potato has cooked for the prescribed 60 minutes, drain all but the final dregs of water, mash with a fork, and set aside.

Place a soup pot on the stove to heat, along with a couple of tablespoons of peanut oil in the bottom of the pot.

Dice the onion and the garlic, and add them into the pot to sauté. Add the onions first, and let them cook until nearly browned before adding in the garlic.

Dice the stew meat into small bite-sized pieces, and add them into the pot once the garlic has been properly cooked. Cook the meat until it has been browned on the outside, and add the beef broth into the pot. Bring the beef broth to a boil as you cut the other vegetables.

Cut the potatoes into medium-sized cubes, and add them into the pot. Peel and cut the potatoes into slices, and add them into the pot.

Let the stew boil for about 20 minutes, or until you're sure the potatoes are nearly cooked. Add in the soy sauce, table wine, and the milk, and let it keep cooking. Add salt and pepper as desired, along with crushed bay leaves for added flavor.

Just 5 minutes before you are about to turn the soup off, add in the mashed potato. Stir the soup well, ensuring that the mashed potato is diluted properly. The starch from the potato will thicken the stew, but it will ensure that the other ingredients aren't overcooked.

Serve with nut bread, and enjoy!

Grain-Free Ideal Breakfast

The ideal way to start the day is with a rich breakfast, but the average breakfast consists of grain-laden toast, pancakes, or other things that are made with grain. If you want the perfect breakfast without adding grain to your diet, this is the recipe for you!

Ingredients:

For this dish, you will need:
3 eggs
2 slices of turkey or Canadian bacon
6 oranges
2 Slices of Nut bread (see recipe above)
Butter
Honey
Coffee

Preparation:

To begin, place a skillet on the stove to heat. Once the skillet is hot, add the bacon and cook until done. Remove the bacon from the stove, and place on a paper towel to drain.

Leaving the bacon grease in the bottom of the pan, let it

reheat until ready for the eggs. Crack one egg into the pan, and crack the other two eggs into a cup -- making sure to get only the egg whites. Add the two egg whites into the pan, and cook the eggs until done as desired. (If you don't like your eggs to be liquid on the top, flip them over and let them sit in the pan for 3 seconds before scooping them onto your plate.)
Add the slices of nut bread onto the plate, along with the Canadian or turkey bacon. Spread butter and honey as desired on the bread, and serve yourself a cup of coffee.

Squeeze the oranges, and enjoy your fresh cup of OJ for the ideal grain-free breakfast!

Dark Chicken Soup

If you're not too particular about the way your soup looks, you'll find that this will be the ideal meal for you! It comes loaded with all the nutrients you need, and there are even a few noodles floating around to help fill you up. All in all, however, it's a nicely low calorie meal - and grain-free as well!

Ingredients

For this dish, you will need:
2 liters of chicken broth
1 bunch of chard
2 carrots
1 bunch of spinach
1 cup of shitake mushrooms
1 pack of shitake mushroom noodles
¼ pound of chicken breast

Preparation:

To begin, place the chard and spinach in a pot with 2 cups of water and 2 cups of chicken stock. Bring the veggies to a boil, and let them cook until they are soft. Pour the soup into the food processor, blend it until it is completely liquefied, and set it aside.

Pour the chicken broth into a pot, and bring it to a boil. Cut the carrots and shitake mushrooms into slices, and add them into the soup. Pour the liquefied dark greens into the pot, and let them cook along with the chicken broth.

In a pan on the side, add a pat of butter into the bottom as the pan heats. Dice the chicken breast into chunks, and let the breast cook until it is browned on the outside. Once it is nearly cooked, pour the chicken and the grease into the soup pot. Let it cook until you're sure the chicken is thoroughly done.

Add the mushroom noodles a few minutes before you want to cook the soup, and follow the cooking instructions on the package. The noodles shouldn't take too long to cook, and you can serve out the soup while it's still piping hot!

Carrot Muffins

These delicious muffins will help you to start the day out right, and you can munch on a couple of them as you head to work. Thanks to the fact that they're completely grain-free, they'll be the perfect option for you!

Ingredients

For this dish, you will need:
¼ teaspoon of baking soda
¼ cup of coconut flour
Cinnamon
3 eggs
Salt
¼ cup of oil
¼ cup of natural molasses
Vanilla
3 carrots
¼ cup of raspberries, blackberries, and black currants

Preparation:

To begin, preheat the oven to about 350 F. This is the perfect temperature for muffins, as it will keep cooking time down without risking burning the muffins.

Combine the baking soda, coconut flour, and a teaspoon of cinnamon in a bowl, and stir it well to ensure that it's properly combined.

In a separate bowl, crack and mix the eggs. Whip them until they are frothy, and pour the oil, molasses, and a teaspoon of vanilla into the mix. Beat well, add a pinch of salt, and combine the wet ingredients with the dry.

Use a whisk to combine the wet and dry ingredients well, and stir until you are sure there are no lumps.

With a bit of butter, grease a muffin tray. You'll get about 12 to 18 medium-sized muffins, though as many as 30 mini muffins. Put the tray into the oven, and cook the muffins for about 30 minutes. Insert a knife into the top of one muffin, and it should come out clean once it's done.

Remove the muffins from the oven, scoop them out of their tray, and set them aside to cool.

Almond and Grilled Chicken Salad

The beauty of salads is that they are some of the best grain-free recipes, and you won't have to worry about getting gluten if you eat a healthy salad. If you want to really go all out with the salad, add nuts and lots of filling veggies! You'll find that it will be tasty and very enjoyable!

Ingredients:

For this dish, you will need:
1 pound of chicken breast
1 head of Romaine or Iceberg lettuce
1 cup of raw almonds
1 cup of raw peanuts
1 cup of dried cranberries
1 apple
½ cup of olive oil
½ cup of apple cider vinegar
1 cup of gluten-free soy sauce
Salt
Sesame seeds

Preparation:

To begin, slice the chicken breast into steaks about ¾

inch thick. You'll get about 3 steaks from a single chicken breast. Place the chicken breast on a grill, and rub a seasoning of salt, pepper, garlic, and Parmesan cheese onto the breast before cooking it. Grill the chicken well on both sides, and make sure that the middle of the chicken is cooked before removing it from the grill. Set the chicken aside.

Soak the lettuce in a bowl of ice cold water, which will make it crunchy and crispy. Once the lettuce has soaked for 30 minutes, use your hands to rip it into bite-sized leaves.

Slice the apple into quarters, cut out the cores, and cut the apple into small chunks. Add the apples into the salad, along with the cranberries.

In a skillet on the stove, place the almonds and peanuts together. The raw nuts will need to be toasted, and they will take about 20 minutes. Make sure to stir them every 5 minutes or so, and keep the heat on medium high to prevent them from burning. Once the almonds and peanuts are toasted, add them into the salad.

Slice the chicken breast into strips, and add them into the salad as well.

Combine the vinegar, soy sauce, and olive oil together, along with a pinch of salt and some black pepper. Pour this mixture over the salad, and sprinkle sesame seeds liberally on top to garnish the salad. It's now ready for you to eat!

Gluten-Free Breakfast Biscuits

There's nothing like a delicious, buttery biscuit to start your day off on the right foot, and these grain-free biscuits will be just what you need to enjoy your morning. They're easy to whip up, and you can take them with you to snack in your car on the way to work.

Ingredients

For this dish, you will need:
2 cups of almond flour
½ teaspoon of baking soda
2 eggs
1 teaspoon of honey
1/3 cup of butter or margarine
Salt

Preparation:

To begin, preheat the oven to about 350 F. This is the temperature that will allow the biscuits to turn golden brown on the outside, but without making the center of the biscuits too dry.

In a bowl, combine the almond flour with the baking soda and a pinch of salt. Stir well to ensure that there are no clumps of baking soda.

In another bowl, crack the eggs and beat them until they are frothy. Add in the butter and the honey, and beat well. You'll want to keep stirring until you have a slightly creamy mixture.

Fold the wet ingredients gently into the dry ones, and mix until you're sure that there are no lumps. You will need to keep stirring as the dough is formed.

Use a piece of greased baking paper to roll the biscuit dough out, and keep rolling until you've flattened the dough to about 1 ½ inches thick. Use a jar with a wide mouth to cut out the biscuits, and keep rolling the dough until you have turned it all into biscuits.

Transfer the biscuits to an oven tray with a piece of greased baking paper, and put the tray into the oven. Let the biscuits cook for about 15 minutes, and keep a close eye on them. You'll notice that the rounded edges of the biscuits will start to brown, and don't let them get too dark before removing them from the oven.

Use a spatula to scrape the biscuits off the greased baking sheet, and set them on a rack to cool. Once they're cool, spread a bit of butter and honey on them, and enjoy!

Nutty Granola

Granola is one of the best breakfasts that you can have, and you'll find that this nutty granola will be just the thing to stoke up your internal furnace first thing in the morning. It's a grain-free breakfast that will kick off your day in style!

Ingredients

For this dish, you will need:
1 cup of steel cut oats
2 cups of almonds
1 cup of amaranth
1 cup of raisins
1 cup of walnuts
1 tablespoon of vanilla
Butter
Cinnamon
Sugar

Preparation:

To begin, place a skillet on the stove to heat. Melt a cup of butter in the bottom of the skillet, and add the oats in once the butter is liquefied completely.

Use a spatula or wooden spoon to roll the oats thoroughly in the butter, and ensure that the oats are properly coated. Remove the skillet from the heat, and transfer the oats into a flat baking tray.

Preheat the oven to 350 F.

Add the raisins into the oats, and cut the almonds and walnuts in half. Add in the amaranth, and sprinkle a bit of sugar, cinnamon, and a few tablespoons of vanilla extract onto the oats. Make sure that the oats are mixed properly, and put the tray into the oven to cook.

Give the oats about 30 minutes to cook at 350 F, but keep checking them to ensure that they don't burn. You'll find that they'll become nice and crunchy once they've cooked properly, but let them cool down before eating them.

Grain-Free Breakfast Bars

Need something quick to munch on as you drive to work in the morning? Don't let the heavy traffic get you down, but make these delicious breakfast bars to help keep your mind off the fact that you're sitting and doing nothing. They're a healthy breakfast that you can enjoy on the go!

Ingredients

For this dish, you will need:
2 cups of almond flour
1/3 teaspoon of baking soda
1/3 cup of grapeseed oil
Vanilla extract
1/3 cup of honey
½ cup of shredded coconut
1/3 cup of raisins
1/3 cup of nuts (your preference)
¼ cup of flax seeds
¼ cup of amaranth
¼ pumpkin seeds

Preparation:

To begin, preheat the oven to 350 F.

In a bowl, combine the almond flour with a pinch of salt and the baking soda. Make sure to mix well, as that will eliminate any lumps of baking soda.

In another bowl, mix the honey with a tablespoon of vanilla and the grapeseed oil. The oil will be a bit hard to mix in, but a bit of effort will yield a properly mixed liquid.

Pour the wet ingredients in with the dry ones, and whisk vigorously to ensure that the wet and dry ingredients combine nicely without any lumps.

Once you're done mixing, add the nuts, seeds, raisins, coconut, and amaranth into the batter. Mix well to distribute the latest additions.

Use a bit of butter to grease the bottom of a baking tray, and pour the mixture into the pan. Place the pan in the oven, and let it cook for about 20 minutes at 350 F. You'll find that it turns a nice golden brown, and it will become very crunchy and a bit hard to cut.

Slice the bars into small pieces, and serve or set aside to eat on the go.

83

Garden-Style Hot Dogs

Hot dogs are one of the most popular American foods around, but the problem is the hot dog bun. If you want to enjoy a classic hot dog in a very unique way, these garden-style hot dogs will be an ideal way for you to eliminate the gluten from your meal.

Ingredients:

For this dish, you will need:
6 hot dogs
6 slices of bacon
1 head of Romaine lettuce
½ tomato
½ onion
Pickle relish
Sauerkraut
Ketchup
Mayo
Mustard
Tabasco sauce

Preparation:

To begin, soak the head of lettuce in ice cold water. The cold water will help to make the lettuce crunchier and crispier, which will make it much easier to eat.

Place a skillet on the stove, and let it heat. As the pan is heating, wrap one strip of bacon around each hotdog. You can hold the bacon in place using toothpicks, but make sure that the toothpicks don't interfere with the cooking process.

Let the hot dogs cook for about 20 minutes on low heat, and turn them regularly to ensure that they don't burn. The grease from the bacon will make them very tasty.

Once they're thoroughly cooked, remove the skillet from the stove, but leave the hot dogs inside.

Remove 12 strips of lettuce, and make 6 stacks of two leaves. Dice the tomato and the onions, making sure that they are very small.

Place a bit of sauerkraut in **the bottom** layer of lettuce, and stack the second leaf on top. Place each hot dog into the top leaf, and add tomato, onion, and pickle relish on top. Add the condiments of your choice, and enjoy the delicious, all-natural hot dog meal!

Grain-Free Mac and Cheese

Mac and Cheese is the quintessential American meal, but egg noodles are made with wheat. Using gluten-free noodles will allow you to still enjoy this delicious dish, but without having to worry about adding grain to your meal!

Ingredients

For this dish, you will need:
2 packs of gluten-free noodles
3 cups of grated cheddar cheese
½ cup of butter
1 ½ cups of milk
2 tablespoons of heavy cream
¼ pound of bacon
1 onion
4 cloves of garlic

Preparation:

To begin, place a skillet on the stove to heat. Add a bit of butter into the bottom of the skillet, and dice the onions as the pan gets hot. Add the onions into the bottom of the pan to sauté, and dice the garlic to add in once the onions begin to brown.

Remove the garlic and onions from the stove once the aroma of the garlic is extracted, and slice the bacon as the skillet heats up once again. Place a pot of water on the stove to boil, which will be for the noodles.

Once the skillet is hot, add the bacon into the pan. Cook until it is nicely browned, and remove from the stove.

Place the onions and garlic back on the stove, and pour the milk and bacon into the pan. Once the milk gets hot, add in the heavy cream and the butter. Bring the ingredients to a boil, and add the cheddar cheese into the mix. Turn the fire off, but leave the pan on the stove.

Boil the noodles, and cook them until they are al dente. Place the noodles back into the pot they were cooked in, add the cheese sauce over the top, garnish with a bit more cheese, and serve while hot!

Almond Raisin Muffins

These muffins are simple and easy to make, but they'll be delicious without a doubt! You can even top them with icing to make delicious cupcakes, or keep them light if you're on a diet! Enjoy them no matter where you are, as they are fantastic.

Ingredients:

For this dish, you will need:
1 cup of flax meal
1 cup of almond flour
1 tablespoon of baking powder
Nutmeg
Cinnamon
½ cup of raisins
1/3 cup of toasted **almonds**
1 stick of butter
Salt
4 eggs
½ cup of sugar
½ cup of buttermilk
2 tablespoons of brown sugar

Preparation:

To begin, you will need to heat the oven to about 375 F. Once the oven is hot, turn it down to 350 F, which is the ideal temperature for baking the muffins.

Combine the baking powder, flax meal, almond flour, and a pinch of salt in a bowl, mixing well to combine. Add a teaspoon each of cinnamon and nutmeg, and stir well.

Combine the butter, eggs, sugar, and milk in a bowl, and beat until the eggs are frothy and the butter is creamy. Using melted butter will make the process a lot quicker, but you can use an egg beater if you don't want to take the time to melt the butter.

Combine the wet and dry ingredients, and mix them well to eliminate any lumps. Add the raisins into the mix. Chop the toasted almonds into small pieces, and add them into the muffin batter as well.

Once the ingredients are all stirred in well, pour the muffin batter into a muffin baking tray. Use paper muffin cups if you want to limit the mess.

Place the muffins in the oven, and let them cook for

roughly 15 to 20 minutes, depending the altitude of your city(it takes longer for things to bake the higher above sea level you are). Insert a toothpick into the top of the muffins when they look cooked, and they are done when the toothpick comes out clean.

Remove the muffins from the tray, set them aside to cool, and serve.

Grain-Free Pizza

Pizza is one of the most popular dishes in the world, but it's hard to make a good pizza without using flour. This pizza is made without wheat, and it's a tasty alternative that gluten-sensitive people can enjoy without worrying about their stomachs acting up.

Ingredients

For this dish, you will need:

1 cup of quinoa flour
1 cup of potato flour
1 cup of almond flour
1 cup of buckwheat
Salt
Xanthan gum
4 teaspoons of dried yeast
Canola or olive oil
Water
Tomato sauce
Cheese
Pizza toppings of your choice

Preparation:

To begin, heat the oven to a toasty 350 F.

Grease some baking sheets with a bit of olive or canola oil, and place them on the trays where you will be cooking your pizza.

Sift the various flours, salt, and baking soda into a bowl, and combine the dry ingredients well. Add the yeast into the mixture.

Mix half a liter of warm water with a couple of tablespoons of olive oil, and add the wet ingredients into the dry ones. Mix the dough until it is properly combined, and set it aside for a few minutes to rise.

Once it has risen, use a spoon to scoop it into your pizza tray. Make a nicely rounded pizza, and put it in the oven to cook until the crust is golden brown.

All that is left to do is to scoop the pizza or tomato sauce onto the top of the crust, add cheese, and top with the ingredients of your choice. Put the crust back into the oven, and cook it until the cheese has properly melted.

Slice, serve, and enjoy!

Your Grain Free Meal Plan

So, you've got all these awesome grain-free recipes to work with! Whether you're trying to lose weight or just stay healthy, eating these foods will help you to keep grain and gluten out of your life. If you want to add these delicious meals to your diet, here is an 11-day meal plan that you can use to incorporate all of these recipes into your life:

Day 1:
Breakfast: Buckwheat Pancakes
Lunch: Eggs and Nut Bread Toast
Dinner: Pad Thai

Day 2:
Breakfast: Gluten Free Waffles
Lunch: Grain-Free Cornbread with Grilled Chicken or Steak, plus plenty of veggies
Dinner: Special K cereal (made with rice rather than wheat flour)

Day 3:
Breakfast: Special K Cereal
Lunch: Stuffed Bell Peppers
Dinner: Chicken with Rice Stuffing

Dessert: Roasted Almond Cookies

Day 4:
Breakfast: Apple Cobbler
Lunch: Asian Sesame Noodles
Dinner: Almond and Grilled Chicken Salad

Day 5:
Breakfast: Breakfast Cereal Sans Gluten
Lunch: Grain Free Breaded Chicken with Nut Bread and veggies
Dinner: Gluten-Free Chicken Noodle Soup with Nut Bread
Dessert: Gluten and Sugar-Free Gingerbread Cake

Day 6:
Breakfast: Carrot Muffins
Lunch: Gluten-Free Turkey Club
Dinner: Curried Quinoa with Chick Peas

Day 7:
Breakfast: Grain-Free Ideal Breakfast
Lunch: Dark Chicken Soup with Nut Bread
Dinner: Grain-Free Mac and Cheese

Day 8:
Breakfast: Gluten-Free Breakfast Biscuits

Lunch: Gluten-Free Potato Beef Stew

Dinner: Shrimp Cakes

Dessert: Gluten-Free Irish Shortbread

Day 9:

Breakfast: Nutty Granola

Lunch: Dark Chicken Soup with Nut Bread

Dinner: Special K Cereal

Day 10:

Breakfast: Breakfast Bars

Lunch: Garden-Style Hot Dogs

Dinner: Sesame Seed Chicken Fried Steak

Day 11:

Breakfast: Almond Flour Muffins

Lunch: Grain-Free Pizza

Dinner: Special K Cereal

The meal plan above doesn't come with the calorie count on each food item, but that's something that won't be as important as the fact that they are all grain-free foods. You can eat them without worrying too much about calories, but try and keep the consumption of these foods to a healthy minimum in order to avoid gaining weight!

All of these recipes can be found online, though some of them are our own original creations. You can probably find similar recipes on websites like AllRecpes.com, About.com, and particularly ElanasPantry.com. They are all recipes that someone made, and we just wanted to share them with you. We've made a few adjustments to the various recipes so that you'll get only our unique grain-free flavor on the recipes, but you'll find that there are many like them. The important thing is that you can enjoy your grain-free cooking and eating, and we wanted to provide you with a recipe book that you can use to prepare delicious meals free of grain and gluten. We apologize if you've seen these recipes elsewhere, and we hope that you enjoy the creations we have presented to you!

[1] http://www.stuff.co.nz/life-style/38883/The-effects-of-gluten-on-health

Section 2: Juicing Guide

More than likely, you have heard all about juicing and juicing diets. However, you may not be familiar with the truth about juicing, especially when it comes to juicing and weight loss. Many people try to start a juicing diet without actually learning what juicing is all about, how long they should being on a juice-only diet and the benefits that juicing has to offer.

If you have considered juicing for weight loss, this guide is for you. This juicing guide offers helpful information on juice, the benefits of juicing and so much more. You will even find some great tips that will make your juice diet even more successful. The best part about this juicing guide is that it is packed with the tastiest, healthiest juicing recipes out there. Whether you enjoy vegetable flavored juices or you like the sweeter juices, you are sure to find great recipes that will fit with your tastes and your lifestyle. Many of the recipes included are very easy to make, especially with the help of a quality juicer.

Do not start your juicing diet until you read this guide. With this guide by your side, you can begin juicing for weight loss, armed with important information and great recipes. Even when you stop juicing for every meal, you can go back to this guide for great juicing recipes that can be used anytime for a great dose of vitamins and minerals.

Chapter 1: What is Juicing?

Before you begin juicing for weight loss, it is important to know more about juicing and how it works. What is juicing? Juicing is simply defined as the process of extracting juices from vegetable of fruit plant tissues. Juicing can be done in several different ways. Some fruits can be juiced by hand, but to get the most juice from most fruits and vegetables, a good juicer is needed.

Many people choose to juice fruits and vegetables because it offers the body many important nutrients in a way that can easily be assimilated by the body. When juicing fruits and veggies at home with a domestic juicer, the produce is prepared and then pushed through the feeding chamber of the juicer. Then the machine uses either a separation or pureeing process to juice the produce.

In most cases, you do not need to peel produce before putting it through the juicer. However, some fruits and vegetables may be exceptions. For example, oranges and other citrus fruits happen to have bitter oils in their peels, which is why it is best to peel them before they are juiced. Fruits and vegetables with a very hard rind, such as squash, pumpkins, watermelon and other similar items of produce will need to have the peel or rind removed to avoid damaging the juicer.

One of the main reasons that juicing has become so popular is because taking in fresh, raw produce is actually much better than taking in vegetables that have been cooked. The juices help to remove toxins and waste from the body, also working to regenerate and repair body tissues. Fresh juices also provide plenty of important enzymes and antioxidants to the body, which can help to improve metabolism, help along metabolic processes and eliminate free radicals within the body.

Juicing not only helps to preserve the important nutrients found in veggies and fruits, but it also allows individuals to take in more produce at one time than they could if they were eating it. A large glass of fruit or vegetable juice includes the juice of more fruits and veggies than you could ever eat at one time.

Of course, while many people can definitely benefit from a juicing diet, it is always a good idea to talk to your doctor before starting any new diet. People who may be taking prescription medications or dealing with an illness need to talk to their doctor before drinking a large quantity of juice, since juices may change the way their body metabolizes the medications they are taking.

For most healthy individuals, juicing provides a healthy, safe way to begin increasing the intake of important nutrients. Even juicing for one meal a day can provide great results.

While some people choose to only juice for one meal each day, others decide to go on a juice diet for a few days where they only take in juices. This may be okay for a few days, but a diet of only juices is usually not a good idea for more than a few days at a time. For the best results, you can drink only juices for a few days and then you can go back to eating a regular healthy diet while drinking a glass of juice for one of your meals each day.

Chapter 2: Benefits of Juicing

Before you decide to start juicing for weight loss, you may want to take a closer look at the benefits juicing can offer you. Juicing has become quite popular because of the many benefits to it. Maybe you have heard other people talk about how great juicing is but wondered if it really can help you. Here is a look at some of the top benefits you can enjoy when you try the juicing diet yourself.

Benefit #1 – Efficiently Consume Large Amounts of Fruits and Veggies

One of the main benefits of juicing is that it allows you to efficiently consume large amounts of fruits and veggies. You should be getting more than five servings of fruits and vegetables each day. The problem is that most people never get that many servings of fruits and veggies. It can be difficult to fit all those fruits and veggies into your meals each day. However, juicing makes it a lot easier for you to get all the fruits and vegetables that your body really needs. In fact, you could actually get all the recommended servings of fruits and veggies in a single glass of juice. This makes it fast and convenient to begin adding more healthy produce to your life on a regular basis.

Benefit #2 – Include a Wide Variety of Fruits and Veggies in Your Diet

Another great benefit of juicing for weight loss is the ability to include a wide variety of fruits and veggies in your diet. If you are eating vegetables and fruits regularly, it is easy to get into a rut. Soon you may find that you are eating the same fruits and veggies on a regular basis. This means that you may not be getting the wide variety of vitamins and minerals that are needed by your body. When you begin juicing, you can include a wider variety of great fruits and veggies in your juices, making sure that you get a wide variety of different nutrients that your body needs.

Some people find that they do not particularly like the flavor of certain fruits and vegetables. When you begin juicing, you can enjoy the benefits of fruits or veggies you do not like as much without having to taste them. Many times you can add certain veggies or fruits to a juice with another fruit or vegetable that has a predominant flavor, overpowering the flavor of the item you do not like. You do not have to avoid certain veggies and fruits just because you do not like their flavor. You can easily add them to juices and get all their benefits without tasting them specifically.

Benefit #3 – Enjoy More Energy

One of the greatest benefits that people often notice after they begin juicing is that they enjoy more energy. One reason that you may experience more energy when juicing is because your body does not have to use very much energy to digest the veggie and fruit juices. The juicers are almost totally digested. You simply drink the juice and your body will not need to use much energy on digestion. Since you are saving all that energy, you will probably notice that your energy levels begin to increase.

Many people that do not get enough fruits and vegetables notice that they feel fatigued on a regular basis. If you are dealing with fatigue and the need to sleep more than usual, juicing may be able to help. After you begin juicing for a few days, you will quickly find that your energy levels begin to skyrocket, which can help improve your life in many different ways.

Benefit #4 – Get Plenty of Chlorophyll From Green Juices

Many of the juicing recipes that you will find in this juicing guide and in other places include produce that contains a lot of chlorophyll. You will especially find a large amount of chlorophyll in the greener juices that include a large amount of greens, such as spinach. Chlorophyll is a great detoxifier and is found naturally in plants. When you begin getting more chlorophyll in your diet, you will find that it helps to eliminate parasites from the body. It also strengthens your body, helps to rebuild your blood cells and helps purify and detoxify your body as well.

Benefit #5 – Detoxify Your Liver for Better Health

You will also find that juicing for weight loss can offer the benefit of detoxifying your liver for better health. Your liver has so many functions that it has to undertake on a regular basis and these functions are very important to the way your body works. One of the most important functions of your liver is to clean out the blood, removing metabolic waste and toxins from the blood. Since most people end up being exposed to many toxins on a regular basis, the liver needs to be in great shape so it can keep your blood as clean as possible.

Some of the best antioxidants that help to cleanse out your liver include vitamin C, beta carotene and vitamin E. Niacin and various B vitamins also help to cleanse the liver as well. Some great veggies that are known to be good for detoxifying the liver include cauliflower, Brussels sprouts and cabbage. Adding some of these veggies to your juices from time to time can help ensure you enjoy this benefit from your juicing.

Benefit #6 – Enjoy Healthier, More Beautiful Skin and Hair

When you begin juicing on a regular basis, you can also enjoy healthier, more beautiful skin and hair. For many people, this benefit is unexpected. When you begin juicing, you will be able to increase your intake of veggies and fruits that contain vitamin E and vitamin C. Both of these vitamins work to help protect your skin from damage when it is exposed to the sun. Some of the best fruits to use to get these vitamins include blueberries and blackberries. In fact, you'll find some recipes in this juicing guide that combine blueberries and blackberries, which can help you get the vitamins you need for healthier skin.

If you are not getting enough riboflavin in your diet, you

can experience hair loss, cracked lips and a variety of different skin problems. Some of the veggies that have a lot of riboflavin in them include spinach and kale, which are found in many of the juicing recipes included. As you begin getting more of this important vitamin, you will notice that your skin begins to get healthier and the hair loss problem may begin to abate as well. Many other vitamins and minerals that you will get while juicing will help improve the health and appearance of your skin and hair as well.

Benefit #7 – Give Your Immune System a Boost

Since so many people today do not get the fruits and vegetables that their body needs, it is no wonder that so many people have weakened immune systems. When you begin juicing on a regular basis, you will enjoy the benefit of giving your immune system a great boost. If you get colds or other illnesses on a regular basis, juicing may be just the thing to help you feel a lot better.

When you begin juicing regularly, you will start getting a wide variety of different antioxidants, which are needed to keep your immune system functioning the way it should. Some of the important antioxidants you will get from veggies and fruits include vitamin E, vitamin A and vitamin C. Phytochemicals are also found in many fruits and vegetables and they come with a variety of great health benefits, giving your immune system and your overall health a good boost.

Benefit #8 – Prevent Cancer

One of the more famous benefits of juicing is the benefit of cancer prevention. Since juicing gives you a wide variety of vitamins, minerals and antioxidants that your body needs, it arms your body to fight off cancer cells. When you juice on a regular basis and ensure you are getting all those important nutrients, you will be going a long way towards reducing your risk of getting cancer in the future.

Interestingly enough, juicing is often recommended to individuals who already have cancer. While it does not miraculously cure cancer right away, the antioxidants help to fight off cancer cells and give the immune system a boost so the body can work to fight off cancer on its own. When used along with other treatments, it can be an excellent method of beating cancer. Of course, if you are being treated for cancer, it is always important to follow the advice of your doctors and make sure you talk to them about juicing to ensure you avoid doing anything that may interfere with other treatments you may be given for cancer.

Benefit #9 – Slow the Aging Process

Last, juicing for weight loss can actually have the benefit of slowing down the aging process. Instead of wasting your money on all those expensive anti-aging creams and lotions, nature can offer you a great anti-aging treatment – fruits and veggies. Drinking fresh juices on a regular basis can provide your body with the nutrients it needs to stay young. Since free radicals are known to cause aging, getting plenty of antioxidants from the juice you drink will help to fight off free radicals, slowing down the aging process. People that get plenty of fruits and vegetables on a regular basis are often able to look younger and they are less likely to deal with health problems that come with aging as well.

Of course, these are only a few of the great benefits you can enjoy when you begin juicing. Juicing may also help to improve heart health, since you are less likely to eat foods that may lead to high blood pressure, high cholesterol and heart disease in the future. Juicing can also help you to lose weight, which is one of the more popular benefits individuals want to experience when they go on a juicing diet. As you begin juicing, you will fill up on low calorie fruits and vegetables in juice form, which will keep you from indulging in other unhealthy foods. Juicing also helps to cleanse out your body, eliminating toxins and waste, which can help you to lose weight as well. Just a few of the other benefits of juicing may include reducing problems with depression, strengthening your bones, improving eye health, rebuilding blood cells, keeping your body pH less acidic and reducing your risk of many different diseases.

Chapter 3: Helpful Tips to Simplify Juicing for Weight Loss

When you begin juicing for weight loss, you want to make sure that you get the best results from your juicing diet. The good news is that there are some great tips out there that can make juicing simpler and tips that can help you ensure you get the best nutrition when you make and drink these juices. To get the tastiest juices and the most benefits from juicing, the following are some top tips to keep in mind as you begin juicing and using the recipes you will find in this book.

Tip #1 – Choose Organic Fruits and Veggies if Possible

One of the best tips to remember when you begin juicing is to choose organic fruits and veggies if possible. Going with organic fruits and veggies helps you avoid pesticides, which you do not want to take in when trying to get all the goodness you can from juicing. Of course, certain fruits and veggies are worse than others when it comes to pesticides. The following fruits and veggies may have thinner skins, which make them more vulnerable to pesticides, so it is better to choose organically grown versions of these items:

- Kale

- Carrots

- Blueberries

- Spinach

- Lettuces

- Cucumbers

- Blueberries

- Strawberries

- Celery

- Collard Greens

If the fruit or vegetable has a thin skin, it is a good idea to choose the organic version of the fruit or veggie when you plan to use them for juicing.

Tip #2 – Learn About Great Additions that Make Juices Taste Better

When you first start juicing, you may find that some of the juices do not taste very good to you, especially those that only have vegetables in them. While you will get used to the taste over time, you can add some simple additions to juices to make them taste better to you. Here are a few of the best additions to add to juices when you need something to make them more palatable for you.

- Cranberries – If you like the flavor of cranberries, they can be added to juices to make them taste a bit better. They work well in green juices, since the cranberry flavor usually overpowers the greens. Not only will the cranberries add great flavor, but they offer a huge amount of antioxidants and phytonutrients as well.

- Coconut – Unsweetened shredded coconut or fresh coconut can be used to offer some flavor to juices as well. Coconut water can also be added to juices to add flavor and dilute them just a bit. Coconut has healthy fats in it, so it tastes good and offers great health benefits too.

- Fresh Ginger – You may notice that many of the juice recipes included in this juicing guide include fresh ginger. This is because ginger adds some great flavor, especially to vegetable juices that may not taste as good. Ginger also works to reduce bad cholesterol levels and offers great cardiovascular health benefits as well.

- Limes and Lemons – Limes and lemons have powerful flavors, which makes them the perfect addition to juices when you want to make them taste a little more palatable. Simple add in half of a lime or a lemon to any juice to improve the flavor. Just make sure you peel the lime or lemon and remove the seeds.

Tip #3 – Always Drink Juices as Soon as You Can Once You Juice Fruits and Veggies

One of the most important tips you can follow as you start juicing is to always drink juices as soon as you can one you have juiced the fruits and veggies. As time goes by, the juice will begin to lose some of its nutritional value. Sometimes the juice will turn a strange color as it begins to oxidize as well, although this does not mean that the juice has gone bad. It is best to drink the juice immediately. If you cannot drink the juice immediately, work to make sure you drink the juice within 24 hours for the best nutrition and taste. Fresh juices do not have any preservatives in them, so they can quickly go bad.

Tip #4 – Try Prepping Produce in Advance for Faster Juicing

Many people avoid juicing because they think that juicing will require a lot of work and time. Juicing actually can take quite a bit of your time, since you have to wash and cut up veggies and fruits before you can juice many of them. Since it can be easy to go off your juicing diet because it all feels like too much work, you may want to try prepping your produce in advance for faster juicing. Try preparing produce by washing it and cutting it up. You can do this a couple times a week so ingredients for juices are readily available. Simple place prepared produce in storage containers or plastic bags, then put them in the refrigerator. Then you can quickly get the ingredients out of the refrigerator and use them when needed. Of course, remember that veggies and fruits can start losing nutrients after you cut them, so if you prep ahead of time, avoid prepping veggies and fruits too far in advance so you avoid losing those important nutrients that your body needs.

Tip #5 – Clean Your Juicer Right Away and Clean Thoroughly

It is important that you clean your juicer right away, making sure that you clean it thoroughly. It is easy to put off cleaning the juicer because you are in a hurry, but this can quickly lead to big problems. If you do not quickly clean out the juice and pulp, it will begin to get sticky. This will make it even more difficult for you to get your juicer clean. If you have a high quality juicer, it should only take a few minutes to clean it when you are done juicing, which will save you a lot of time later on. If your juicer has a metal grater, one of the best tips for cleaning it is to keep a toothbrush around to get it clean.

Tip #6 – If You Do Store Juice, Store Carefully

While it is best to drink your juices quickly, you can store them. However, if you are going to store juices, make sure you store them carefully. Juices are best right away, but you can keep them stored for about 24 hours without too much of a problem. For the best results, make sure you place juice in a glass jar – avoid putting juice in a plastic container. Make sure that the jar has a lid that is airtight and fill the jar with juice right up to the top so you avoid having too much oxygen in the jar, which can damage your juice. Once you have the juice in the jar, make sure it is put in your refrigerator and keep it there until you are ready to drink the juice.

Tip #7 – Always Take the Time to Wash Produce

Always make sure you take the time to wash your produce thoroughly before you juice it. Fruit and vegetables may have contaminants on the outside, which you need to wash away to avoid contaminating your fruit. Even if you are going to remove the peeling or the rind, you still need to wash the produce well. Contamination can still occur if the skin or rind is removed.

Tip #8 – Avoid Peeling Fruits and Veggies that Can Be Eaten with the Skin

If you can eat the fruit or vegetable with the skin on, leave the skin on when you juice them. Many fruits and vegetables contain a large amount of nutrients within their skins, so removing the skins means that you are losing out on some great nutrition. For example, you can leave the skin on cucumbers, apples and even carrots when you are ready to juice them. Just make sure you wash them very well before juicing. Pay attention to the recipes within this juicing guide, since they will tell you when it is okay to leave the skin on the fruits or vegetables that go in the juice.

Tip #9 – Do Not Ruin Your Juice by Adding Sugar – There are Better Ways to Sweeten Juices

When you go on a juicing diet to lose weight, you are working to get away from sugar and processed foods. Do not ruin your juice by adding sugar to the juice if you think it needs a little sweetness. The great news is that there are many better ways that you can sweeten the juices a bit if you think they need it. For example, instead of sugar, a sugar alternative like Stevia, which happens to be all natural, can add some sweetness to the juice. A touch of honey can add some sweetness in a natural way as well. In many cases, just adding a sweet fruit to the juice can help you ensure that you get plenty of sweet flavor in the juice. There is never a need to add any sugar to these juice recipes.

Chapter 4: Delicious Juicing Recipes for Any Meal

If you're following the a juicing diet, you'll find that you can use juicing recipes for any meal or snack during the day. Juicing for weight loss can be extremely effective, but you want to ensure you have a wide variety of juices to enjoy so you don't get bored. The following are some wonderful recipes. Some include fruits, others are primarily made up of veggies and some even include both fruits and vegetables. You're sure to find some great juicing recipes that will tempt your taste buds while helping you lose some weight.

Orange Mango Juice Recipe

This juice combines together the delicious flavors of oranges and mangos. The addition of some kale leaves provides an extra nutritional punch when you consume this juice. You'll be able to make this juice very quickly and it's an especially tasty treat when you first get up in the morning. Add a little ice to make it extra cold and refreshing.

What You'll Need:

1 large mango
4 medium oranges
3-4 leaves of kale

How to Make It:

Wash the mango before using. Remove the skin from the mango, since some individuals may have a bad reaction to some of the chemicals naturally found in the mango's skin. Cut the pit of the mango out, then cut the mango into medium sized chunks.

Peel all four oranges. Break the oranges into 4-5 big sections that can easily be fed into the juice.

Was the kale leaves and shake them dry or dry with a paper towel.

Place mango chunks, orange sections and kale leave in a juice. Juice ingredients. Makes 1-2 servings. Drink immediately for the best taste.

Refreshing Red Pepper and Basil Juice Recipe

Along with refreshing, tasty red bell pepper, this juice is packed with great veggies. It includes cucumbers, broccoli, carrot, celery and chia seeds, which pack in plenty of great nutrients. The basil really gives the flavor a boost, as does the lime. The tabasco adds a kick, but you can eliminate the tabasco if you don't like it.

What You'll Need:

1 large bunch of broccoli
1 handful of fresh basil leaves
1 carrot, small
1 small cucumber
1 red bell pepper, large
½ lime, with the rind
2 teaspoons of chia seeds
2 celery stalks
½ cup of Jicama with the skin
Tabasco sauce to taste (optional)

How to Make It:

Wash broccoli, basil leaves, carrot, cucumber, red bell pepper, celery and Jicama.

Remove pepper top, seeds and innards from the red bell pepper. Cut broccoli into chunks. Peel carrot and cut carrot into chunks. Leave peeling on cucumber but cut cucumber into chunks that will fit into your juicer. Chop celery into chunks as well.

Place broccoli, basil leaves, carrot, cucumber, bell pepper, lime, celery stalks and Jicama into the juicer. Juice until finished. Place juice in a bottle or pitcher. Add tabasco if desired and chia seeds. Mix well. Serve immediately.

Lime Spinach Juice Recipe

All the spinach in this juice offers many great nutrients your body needs, such as potassium and iron. The baby carrots add even more vitamins and minerals that are important. The lime and green apple added to the juice provide a delicious flavor that will make you wish you doubled this recipe.

What You'll Need:

1 medium green apple
1 large cucumber
5-6 baby carrots
2 large handfuls of spinach
1 lime

How to Make It:

Wash the green apple, cutting it into chunks, leaving skin on the apple. Wash cucumber and leave it's skin on too, cutting into chunks. Wash spinach carefully, allowing to drain in a colander. Wash lime, remove the skin and then cut up the lime into chunks.

Add apple chunks, cucumber chunks, carrots, spinach and lime chunks into the juicer. Juice the ingredients.

Serve juice right away.

NOTE: If you like your juice a bit sweeter, simply add another apple to the juice for some extra sweetness.

Wild Edible Greens Juice Recipe

If you have a lot of wild, edible greens around your home, these fresh greens can be added to your juice for a healthy, delicious juice. Just make sure you know which greens are edible, since you want to avoid eating anything that could be dangerous. Have fun finding out about fresh wild greens. You can look online or even buy a book that will help you to identify greens that you can eat.

What You'll Need:

½ cucumber
1 large lemon
1 ½ pounds of fresh wild greens (such as sow thistle, chick weed, yellow dock, dandelion or miner's lettuce)
1 inch piece of fresh ginger root
3-4 bok choy stalks
6 celery tops

How to Make It:

Start by washing all the fresh wile greens you have collected, allowing them to drain in a colander before using them in the juice. Wash cucumber, lemon, bok choy and celery tops as well. Leave the skin on the cucumber, cutting it up into pieces that will easily fit in your juicer. Chop bok choy stalks into smaller pieces and cut up celery tops if needed.

Add all ingredients to the juicer, juicing until complete. Makes about 24 ounces of wild edible greens juice, which is about two servings. Drink the juice immediately.

Tasty Morning Apple and Carrot Juice Recipe

This delicious juice is a wonderful juice to make in the morning for a great pick me up. It's tasty and packed with great nutrients to help fuel you through the day. The beet adds some great vitamins and minerals, but you won't taste it with the green apples in the juice, offering a nice sweet and tart flavor.

What You'll Need:

1/2 beet
2 medium green apples
1 stalk of celery with leaves
2 medium sized carrots

How to Make It:

Wash the apples, celery and carrots. Cut a beet in half, peeling carefully and cutting into chunks. Leave the peeling on the apples, but core the apple and then cut it into pieces. The celery should be cut up as well. Peel carrots, cutting into large pieces.

Place the beet, apples, celery and carrots into a juicer and then process. Serve the juice up right away for a great way to start the morning.

Carrot Citrus Twist Juice Recipe

The carrots in this delicious juice recipe pack great nutrients, offering one of the best ways to get vitamin A. Some of the other important minerals carrots provide include copper, potassium, calcium and iron. While carrot juice tastes great by itself, adding the citrus to the recipe really gives it a tangy, sweet twist. Not only do the oranges add great flavor, but they add a huge amount of vitamin C to your juice as well. Try this delicious juice recipe over ice. It makes a great juice to drink for breakfast.

What You'll Need:

2 large oranges, peeled and seeded
8 large carrots, unpeeled

How to Make It:

Start by peeling the oranges, making sure you remove any seeds. Break up the oranges into large sections so they will fit into your juicer.

Wash the carrots well, removing any dirt. However, leave the skin on the carrots, since the skin is packed with great nutrients. Cut the tops off the carrots. Cut carrots into chunks.

Place oranges and carrots into the juicer, juicing. Makes 2 glasses of juice.

Tangy Grapefruit Carrot Juice Recipe

With eight carrots in this recipe, you'll get a large dose of vitamin A and other essential vitamins and minerals your body needs. You get a tangy surprise to this juice by adding the grapefruit. Grapefruits also pack in plenty of great nutrients, such as vitamin C. Some studies even show that grapefruit can even help you boost your weight loss efforts. While the mint is optional in this juice recipe, it really adds to the flavor. Mint also helps to reduce stomach problems and may help prevent cancer as well.

What You'll Need:

2 medium grapefruits
8 unpeeled large carrots
1 mint sprig, fresh (optional)

How to Make It:

Get started by washing the grapefruits, then peeling it and removing any seeds. Break the grapefruits into large sections to make them easily fit into your juicer. Wash the carrots well, but leave the peels on. Take the tops off the carrots as well. Take time to wash the mint before using.

Start by juicing the mint, then run the grapefruit and carrots through the juicer, which should bring out the any mint juice left in the juicer. Serve the juice immediately.

For a nice, refreshing twist, add the juice to a blender, adding in some ice. Blend until you have a slushy mixture. This cold, delicious twist to the juice recipe is wonderful on a very hot day.

Very Veggie Blast Juice Recipe

This juice recipe is packed with many great veggies, including carrots, celery, kale, radishes, tomatoes, bell peppers and more. The apple that is added to the mix adds some sweetness and the fresh ginger root gives the juice a nice kick. You'll get a wide ranges of vitamins and minerals when you whip up this delicious juice recipe.

What You'll Need:

1 red bell pepper

3 celery stalks

1 medium tomato

1 beet

2 inches of turmeric root

½ bunch of kale

2-3 inch chunk of Daikon radish

1 large carrot

3-4 leaves of basil

½ bunch of fresh cilantro

1 green apple

1 inch of fresh ginger root

How to Make It:

Begin by washing the bell pepper, celery stalks, tomato, beet, kale, radish, carrot, basil leaves, cilantro and apple. Remove seeds and top from the pepper, cutting pepper into large chunks. Chop celery stalks into chunks. Cut the tomato into quarters. Cut the beet into quarters or smaller to make it fit through your juicer. Remove the top of the carrot, but leave peeling on the carrot. Core the green apple and cut into chunks.

Process all the ingredients through a juicer. When juicing is complete, take the leftover pulp and process it in the juicer again. Serve juice right away and avoid saving leftovers.

Bone Building Kale Juice Recipe

Keeping your bones healthy and strong is important, and this juice recipe is packed with great ingredients that include vitamins and minerals that will help keep bones healthy. The kale included in the juice includes vitamin K, vitamin A, vitamin C, iron, calcium and beta carotene. The carrots offer more beta carotene and vitamin A. The apple adds some fiber and sweetness to the juice and even the parsley offers many great health benefits as well.

What You'll Need:

5 large kale leaves
1 medium green apple
5 large carrots
4-6 sprigs of parsley

How to Make It:

Wash the kale leaves and the parsley sprigs and allow them to drain in a colander. Wash the carrots well, removing any dirt. Cut the tops off the carrots but leave the peelings on them. Wash the apple, then core the apple. Leave the apple skin in place, since it includes great nutrients.

Process the kale leaves, green apple, carrots and parsley in the juicer. Cut ingredients into chunks if needed to fit through the juicer. After ingredients are juiced, drink the juice immediately for the best taste and nutritional punch.

*NOTE: a masticating juicer works best for this recipe and others that include leafy greens

Iron Packed Spinach Broccoli Juice Recipe

Getting plenty of iron in your diet is important, since iron helps with the production of red blood cells and the transportation of oxygen throughout your body. If you are not getting enough iron, you could experience symptoms that include headaches, low energy, weak hair and fingernails, shortness of breath and rapid heartbeat. This juice is made with iron packed veggies that help you get a great dose of iron when you drink this juice. Drinking it on a regular basis can help improve your iron levels and the ingredients also provide other important nutrients your body needs as well.

What You'll Need:

2 stalks of broccoli
2 beetroots
8-10 large spinach leaves

How to Make It:

Start by washing the beetroots and the broccoli stalks. Wash the spinach leaves and allow them to drain before juicing. Cut the beetroots and broccoli stalks into large pieces that will go through your juicer.

Juice the ingredients. Enjoy this juice immediately for the best benefits. Makes about 2 servings.

Citrus and Cabbage Juice Recipe

This delicious juice recipe includes a variety of different vegetables and fruits, which means you'll get plenty of nutrients when you drink it. It makes a great juice to start out your day with. The spinach and beetroot offer plenty of iron and the citrus offers a great supply of vitamin C, which helps your body better use the iron. The cabbage included in the juice provides many health benefits as well, including slowing down the aging process and helping to prevent certain types of cancer. All the citrus fruits included in this recipe means you will get a sweet, tangy flavor and you probably will not taste the cabbage and other veggies at all.

What You'll Need:

¼ head of cabbage
5-6 leaves of spinach
1 kiwifruit
½ a large grapefruit
½ of a medium beetroot
1 stalk of broccoli
1 large orange
½ of a large lemon
1 inch piece of fresh ginger

How to Make It:

Wash the cabbage and spinach leaves, allowing them to drain in a colander before juicing. Peel the kiwifruit, grapefruit, orange and lemon. Make sure that you remove any seeds in the grapefruit, orange and lemon. Was the beetroot and broccoli.

Begin by juicing the cabbage, spinach and broccoli. Once they are done juicing, add the ginger and the citrus fruits. When complete, make sure everything is mixed together well. This makes enough juice for at least two servings, so enjoy sharing this juice with a friend or family member instead of saving it.

Cucumber and Tomato Immune Boosting Juice Recipe

Juicing not only provides a great way to lose some weight, but it also can help you boost your immune system as well. This juice in particular is filled with ingredients that will give your immune system a nice boost. The parsley has high iron content and is a great antioxidant that helps to fight off bacteria. The garlic has antibacterial and antiseptic properties, which can boost your immune system as well. Lycopene comes from the tomatoes in the juice, which can help prevent certain types of cancer. While this is not a sweet juice, it has a nice, wholesome, savory taste that you are sure to enjoy.

What You'll Need:

1 large handful of fresh parsley

½ cucumber, unpeeled

2 large tomatoes

1 clove of garlic, peeled

2 stalks of celery

1/8 of a medium sized onion (try a sweet onion like a Vidalia for better flavor)

How to Make It:

Wash the parsley carefully and allow to drain. Wash the cucumber and leave the peeling on, since it includes important nutrients. Wash tomatoes, cutting into large chunks. Peel the garlic clove. Wash celery and onion. Cut celery into chunks.

Add the parsley to the juicer first, since parsley does not provide a whole lot of juice. After juicing the parsley, juice the cucumber, tomatoes, garlic, celery and onion. Pour the mixture into a glass, making sure it is well mixed up. Drink immediate for the best results. Makes a single serving of juice.

Sweet Pineapple Watermelon Juice Recipe

Watermelon is such a sweet, refreshing fruit, especially on a hot day. It is high in vitamin B6, which is known to help reduce tension. If you have a tough day ahead, this juice a great choice. The lemon and pineapple add even more nutrients that are important and plenty of delicious flavor as well. With all the sweetness of this juice, you may want to serve it up over ice for a cool, sweet treat that is actually good for you.

What You'll Need:

¼ of a watermelon
½ of a pineapple
½ of a lemon

How to Make It:

Remove the rind from the watermelon. If the watermelon has seeds, make sure that you remove them before you begin juicing. Remove the rind from the pineapple and peel the lemon. Remove any seeds from the lemon as well. Cut the watermelon and the pineapple into manageable chunks so they are easier for you to juice.

Juice the watermelon, pineapple and lemon. Once you are done juicing, mix the juice well to ensure it is well combined. Drink right away. Serve it over some ice or add it to the blender with a cup or so of ice and blend for a frosty, delicious drink.

Kiwi Strawberry Energy Boosting Juice Recipe

If you need a great boost of energy, try this delicious kiwi strawberry energy boosting juice recipe. It can be a great way to start your day or you can make this juice to drink before you work out. This way you have plenty of energy to help you make the most of your exercise routine. The kiwi, apple, strawberries and lime all give this juice a sweet taste. If you want to make it a little sweeter, you can also mix in just a bit of organic Stevia to the juice before you drink it.

What You'll Need:

½ of a lime
6 large strawberries
4 large kale leaves
2 kiwis, peeled
2 medium green apples
Pinch of organic Stevia (optional)

How to Make It:

Peel the lime and remove and seeds. Wash strawberries, removing the tops. Wash the kale leaves and allow to drain. Wash and peel the kiwis. Wash and then core the apples, leaving on the peels.

Juice the lime, strawberries, kale leaves, kiwis and green apples. Pour into a glass and enjoy this sweet drink right away. Enjoy the natural rush of energy.

Citrus, Apple, Pear Juice Recipe

Pears are a sweet, delicious fruit that happens to be rich in vitamin K, vitamin C and vitamin A. This fruit is also known to help improve digestion, which is important for cleansing out the body. Combined with the tartness of green apples and delicious citrus fruits, this juice will make your taste buds sing. Have fun trying the recipes with several different types of pears, such as red Anjou pears, Bosc pears or the wonderful Asian pears.

What You'll Need:

2 medium pears (choose the pear of your choice)
2 large carrots
1 large orange
1 medium tangerine
1 large granny smith apple

How to Make It:

Wash the pears, removing the core and seeds; however, the peeling can be left on the pears. The carrots should be washed and topped, leaving the peels. Peel the orange and tangerine after washing them, breaking into large sections. Wash and then core the granny smith apple, leaving the peel on the apple as well.

Run the pears, carrots, orange, tangerine and apple through the juicer. Pour the juice over ice and drink it right away. If the juice is too thick or strong, you can always add a bit of water to get the juice to your desired consistency and taste.

Beta Carotene Deluxe Juice Recipe

You are guaranteed to get a huge dose of beta carotene when you drink this delicious juice. It includes delicious cantaloupe, which is known to include many different vitamins and minerals essential to your body. Vitamin C and vitamin A are just a few of the important vitamins included in cantaloupe. You will also find that it includes a high concentration of potassium as well.

What You'll Need:

1 medium cantaloupe
4 medium sized carrots
1 large sweet potato

How to Make It:

Wash the cantaloupe and then remove the rind. However, you should try to leave a bit of the greenish rind behind to juice, since it offers many great nutrients. Wash the carrots and top them, leaving the peelings. Wash the sweet potato thoroughly, leaving the peel on the sweet potato as well.

Juice the cantaloupe, carrots and sweet potato. Make sure the juice is well mixed to combine the flavors. Drink immediate for a large amount of beta carotene.

Antioxidant Mixed Berry Juice Recipe

When it comes to getting antioxidants, berries happen to have more antioxidants than most other fruits. Antioxidants found in the berries help to protect the body against damage from free radicals. Many berries can also aid in weight loss, since raspberries are known to include ketones that help burn off fat and strawberries can help keep blood sugar levels stable. Strawberries include more than 100% of the daily value of vitamin C and other berries like blackberries and blueberries include a high amount of vitamin C as well. The addition of mango to this juice recipe adds even more vitamin C and a nice dose of vitamin A as well. The apples add some great fiber, which will fill you up and help keep your digestive system working the way it should. This juice will taste wonderful when blended with some ice or simply served over ice, offering a chilly, refreshing, healthy drink that will taste great at any time of day.

What You'll Need:

1 cup of blueberries
1 cup of strawberries
½ cup of raspberries
½ cup of blackberries

½ cup of cubed mango

1 green apple

How to Make It:

Wash the blueberries, strawberries, raspberries and blackberries. Remove the stems from the strawberries. Wash a mango and peel it, cubing up a ½ cup of the mango. Save the rest of the mango for another juicing recipe. Wash the apple and then core it and remove its seeds. Leave the apple peeling in place.

Pass the blueberries, strawberries, raspberries, blackberries, mango and apple through a juicer. Juice the apple last, since it will help clean out some of the berry juices left behind. Pour over ice or mix in a blender with a cup of ice. Drink immediately for a nice dose of antioxidants.

Coconut Mango Tropical Delight Juice Recipe

Mangos have a delicious, sweet flavor. Not only do they taste great, but they include high amounts of vitamin C and pectin as well, which can help lower blood pressure and cholesterol. The vitamin A included in mangos can help keep eyes healthy as well. The one problem people often have with mangos is figuring out if they are ripe or not. A ripe mango should have a bit of give to the outside skin and should have a nice, sweet scent as well. The addition of coconut water and several tropical fruits makes this juice recipe a delight for your taste buds.

What You'll Need:

1 large mango, prepared
2 medium oranges
2 cups of pineapple, cubed
1 lime
½ inch piece of fresh ginger
Coconut water, to your own taste

How to Make It:

To prepare the mango for juicing, start by washing the skin carefully to ensure the flesh is not contaminated. The pit must be removed from the mango, which can be done by slicing around the pit and pulling sections apart to pop out the pit. Use a sharp knife to score the mango flesh, then scooping out the flesh with a spoon, ensuring the rind is left behind.

Wash and peel the oranges and ensure pineapple is cubed small enough to easily go through the juicer. Peel the lime and remove any seeds. Wash ginger before juicing as well.

Run the mango flesh, oranges, pineapple, lime and ginger through the juicer. Mix the finished juice with some coconut water until you have the flavor you prefer. Drink at room temperature or pour over ice for a refreshing tropical treat.

Pear, Apple, Blueberry Juice Recipe

Blueberries are not just wonderfully juicy and sweet, but these small berries include a high amount of antioxidants as well. This fruit is known to help reduce the risk of inflammation and may help protect against certain types of cancer as well. Since these berries have such thin skin, it is a good idea to use organic berries whenever possible. This juice recipe adds the delicate flavor of pears and the sweet, tartness of granny smith apples as well, making a juice that is packed with flavor and great nutrients for the body. Enjoy changing up the flavor a bit by using different kinds of pears in the juice.

What You'll Need:

1 cup of blueberries
½ cup of strawberries
½ cup of blackberries
1 pear, any kind
2 granny smith apples

How to Make It:

Wash the blueberries, strawberries and blackberries. Remove the tops from the strawberries. Wash the pear and the apple. Remove the core and stem from the pear, cutting the pear into large chunks. Core the apple, leave the skin on and then cut the apple into large pieces.

Run the blueberries, strawberries and blackberries through the juicer first. Then, run the pear and apples through the juicer, cleaning out the berry juices when they go through the juicer. Fill a glass with ice cubes and pour juice over the ice. Drink the juice right away to get the most nutrients from the ingredients.

Carrot and Cucumber Broccoli Juice Recipe

The broccoli included in this juice is high in both vitamin C and vitamin E, which are known to help support the immune system. This vegetable also has anti-carcinogenic properties and some evidence shows that broccoli may help prevent cancer. Although broccoli offers great nutrition, it is low in calories, which means it is a great addition to your juices if you are trying to lose weight. When juicing the broccoli, make sure you juice the head and the stalks for the nutrition. The carrots and cucumbers add more flavor and nutrition to this juice.

What You'll Need:

1 large cucumber
3 stalks of celery, including the leaves
1 stalk of broccoli, including the head and the stalk
3 large carrots

How to Make It:

Begin by washing the cucumber, celery and carrots. Clean the broccoli very well, since the head often traps bacteria and dirt. Leave the peeling on the cucumber and cut into large chunks. Cut the celery into chunks as well. Do not peel the carrots, but make sure you remove the tops, then cutting the carrots into large pieces. Cut the broccoli into small enough pieces to easily fit into your juicer.

Run the cucumber, celery, broccoli and carrots through your juicer. When done juicing, serve up the juice right away. This juice is usually best at room temperature.

Delicious Tropical Papaya and Pineapple Juice Recipe

Since pineapple has such a high water content, it is a great fruit to use when juicing, providing plenty of juice. Pineapple is high in minerals like manganese and vitamins, such as vitamin C. The sweetness of the pineapple is delicious with other fruits that are more tart. To get the most out of your pineapple when juicing, add the core of the pineapple to the juicer as well, since it offers a lot of bromelain. The other tropical fruits in this juice, such as the papaya, guava and mango, really add a complexity of flavors to this juice.

What You'll Need:

1 large orange, peeled
1 cup of papaya, cubed
1 cup of pineapple, cubed
1 guava
½ of a large mango

How to Make It:

Rinse off the orange and then peel it, removing any seeds. Break the orange up into large sections. Prepare a papaya and cube up a cup of it for the juice. Cube up a cup of pineapple, including some of the core. Prepare the guava for juicing. Wash the mango, removing the pit and using half of the mango flesh for this recipe. Save the rest of the mango for another juice recipe.

Run the orange, papaya, pineapple, guava and mango through the juicer. Fill a large glass with crushed ice, pouring the juice over the ice. Serve the juice immediately for the best flavor and nutrition. This juice is so delicious that you may want to double the recipe and share some with a friend.

Pineapple and Kale Detoxifying Juice Recipe

This recipe includes all the benefits of pineapple, including bromelain, vitamin C and manganese. It also includes great nutrition from the kale included, as well as wonderful nutrients from the cucumber, lemon and mint. This juice is a great detoxifying recipe. For the best results, make this recipe and drink the juice throughout an entire day. Refrigerate the juice until needed but make sure all the juice is consumed within 24 hours or less.

What You'll Need:

2 large cucumbers, unpeeled
½ of a lemon, peeled and seeded
½ cup of pineapple, including the core
1 large bunch of mint
1 large bunch of kale, stems removed
¼ inch of fresh ginger

How to Make It:

Rinse the cucumber thoroughly, leaving the peelings in place. Chunk the cucumbers into large pieces. Wash the lemon, peel it and then remove any seeds. Prepare the pineapple, ensuring it is cubed and include a bit of the core with the pineapple chunks. Wash the mint leaves and kale in a colander, allowing to drain thoroughly before juicing. Wash the ginger as well.

Process the cucumbers, lemon, pineapple, mint, kale and ginger in the juicer. Place the juice in a pitcher. Drink one cup of the juice right away. Store leftovers in the refrigerator and consume throughout the day. Ensure all the juice is consumed within one day for the best results.

Fruity Cleansing Juice Recipe

Many people choose to go on the juicing diet to cleanse their body and lose weight. While there are many delicious juicing recipes that can be used to accomplish these goals, this fruity cleansing recipe is a delicious, nutritious way to begin cleansing the body. All the fruits included provide plenty of vitamins and minerals, not to mention you are sure to appreciate the delicious, fruity flavor as well.

What You'll Need:

1 granny smith apple
½ cup of blueberries
½ cup of raspberries
2 large peaches
2 large oranges, peeled

How to Make It:

To begin making the fruity cleansing juice recipe, start by washing the granny smith apple, the blueberries, raspberries, peaches and oranges. After all the fruits have been washed, remove the core and seeds from the apple, leaving the peeling intact. Remove the seeds from the peaches, but leave the peach skins intact. Peel the oranges, removing any seeds. Cut the apple and peaches into large pieces and break the oranges into large sections.

Process the blueberries, raspberries, peaches and oranges in a juicer. Run the apple pieces through the juicer last. Drink the juice right away. For the best cleansing results, drink the juice while it is at room temperature.

Go Green Spinach and Cucumber Juice Recipe

This delicious juice recipe is all about the greens. It has cucumbers, parsley, spinach, celery and even a granny smith apple in it. All the spinach offers a great dose of potassium and iron. Not only does this juice provide many essential vitamins and minerals that your body needs, but also the juice is also great for detoxifying your body. If you do not like the flavor, you can always add a second apple to the recipe to add some extra sweetness.

What You'll Need:

2 large handfuls of baby spinach
1 stalk of celery, with the leaves
1 large cucumber
1 large handful of fresh parsley
1 large granny smith apple

How to Make It:

Use a colander and rinse the baby spinach and parsley, allowing the leaves to drain in the colander until they are well drained. Wash the celery, cucumber and the apple. Chop the celery into large pieces. Leave the peeling on the cucumber and chop it into large chunks.

Core the apple, making sure all seeds are removed. Do not remove the peel. Cut the apple into pieces.

Run the spinach and parsley through the juicer first, since they do not provide as much juice. Then, run the celery, cucumber and apple through the juicer last. Blend together all the juices. Serve this juice over some ice in a tall glass. Enjoy immediately.

Spinach and Cinnamon Metabolism Booster Juice Recipe

If you are juicing for weight loss, you want to consume juices that will give your metabolism a nice boost. After all, if you have been eating processed foods for many years, your metabolism may have slowed down, which can make it more difficult for you to lose weight. This recipe will help give your metabolism a nice boost and it is packed with ingredients that help to blast away fat as well. The cinnamon adds a nice touch to the juice and is known to help stabilize blood sugar levels.

What You'll Need:

1 cup of spinach leaves
4 large carrots, unpeeled
1 lemon
1 stalk of celery with the leaves
¼ teaspoon of cinnamon
1 granny smith green apple

How to Make It:

Start out by placing the spinach leaves in a colander, rinsing them very well before using. Allow to drain a bit before juicing them. Wash the carrots, topping them but leaving the peelings on them. The lemon should be peeled and the seeds removed after washing it. Wash the celery and apple as well. Cut the celery into big pieces. Core the apple and then cut into pieces too.

Run the spinach leaves from the juicer first. Then run the carrots, celery, lemon and apple through your juicer. After juicing, mix the cinnamon into the juice, stirring well to combine. If the lemon makes the juice a bit tart, use a bit of purified water to dilute it a bit before drinking. Drink right away and enjoy the boost to your metabolism.

Green Juice with a Hint of Sweetness Recipe

This is a green juice recipe that includes all green ingredients. While it includes greens like kale, romaine and parsley, the apple adds a touch of sweetness to the juice. With all the greens in the juice, this is a drink that is packed with vitamins and minerals that will fuel your body and offer plenty of energy for your day. Try drinking this juice if you are feeling a bit tired or you feel like your immune system needs a boost.

What You'll Need:

3 stalks of celery
2 cups of fresh parsley
1 granny smith apple
2 cups of kale leaves
1 large cucumber
3 cups of romaine lettuce

How to Make It:

The celery, cucumber and apple should all be washed. The parsley, kale and romaine leaves can be washed in a colander and allowed to drain and dry a bit before you place them in a juicer.

Cut the celery and cucumber into chunks, leaving the peeling on the cucumber. Do not peel the apple, but core it and then cut into large apple chunks.

Process the parsley, kale leaves and romaine lettuce in the juicer first. Then run the celery, apple and cucumber through the juicer. Make sure you mix up the juicer very well to ensure you get the hint of sweetness throughout the entire batch of juice. Serve the juice immediately.

Potassium Delight Spinach Juice Recipe

Potassium is an important nutrient that your body needs. If you do not get enough potassium, you may suffer from muscle cramps and other symptoms. This juice can help you ensure that you are getting enough potassium in your diet, since the spinach is extremely high in potassium. The lemon juice adds some great flavor to the juice.

What You'll Need:

1 granny smith or other green apple
1 stalk of celery
1 handful of fresh baby spinach leaves
4 medium carrots, tops and greens removed
½ lemon
1 handful of fresh parsley

How to Make It:

Thoroughly rinse off the apple, celery, carrots and lemon. Use a colander to rinse the baby spinach leaves and parsley, letting the leaves dry some before using them in the juice. Without removing the peeling, core the apple and cut into quarters. Cut the celery into large pieces. Remove the carrot tops and chop carrots into big chunks. Peel the lemon and ensure any seeds have been removed before juicing.

Juice the parsley and the spinach leaves first. Place the apple, celery, lemon and carrots in the juicer. Juice. Ensure the juice is well mixed together for the best flavor. Serve the juice right away.

V-8 Flavored Juice Recipe

If you like the flavor of V-8 juice, this juice recipe is a great choice for you to try. You get the great flavor of the juice with even more vegetables and you can be sure of the ingredients going into the juice. With all the great vegetables in this juice, it has plenty of great flavor. The hot sauce really adds a nice pop to the juice, although it is optional and you do not have to add it if you do not like hot sauce. Whip this juice up on a hot day and enjoy the taste of vegetable goodness while getting all those important vitamins and other needed nutrients.

What You'll Need:

2 large tomatoes

2 medium carrots

2 teaspoons of lemon juice

¼ cup of water

1 large handful of spinach leaves

2 stalks of celery

2 cloves of garlic

¼ of a sweet Vidalia onion or other sweet onion

Hot sauce to taste (optional)

How to Make It:

Thoroughly wash the tomatoes, carrots, celery and onion. Rinse leaves well within a colander and let them drain. Peel the garlic cloves. Chop tomatoes into quarters or eights, making sure they will fit in the juicers. Chop the carrots, celery and onion into large chunks.

Place the spinach in the juicer and process. Add the tomatoes, carrots, celery, garlic and onion in the juicer and juice. Once the juice is complete, add the lemon juice and water. Mix together until well combined. Add the hot sauce to the juice to your own taste. Serve the juice right away and enjoy the nice combination of vegetable flavors.

Blueberry and Pomegranate Fruit Juice Recipe

Pomegranates are very high in antioxidants and vitamins, such as vitamin C. This fruit is known to help lower cholesterol and reduce the risk of heart disease. While pomegranates are delicious, preparing them for juicing can be a bit perplexing. Instead of eating the flesh of the pomegranate, the seeds of the fruit are actually eaten instead. This juice recipe not only includes pomegranates, but it includes blueberries and grapes as well, which add even more vitamins and antioxidants to this incredibly healthy and delicious juice. The wonderful sweetness makes it a great juice to enjoy when you want something sweet and refreshing.

What You'll Need:

1 cup of fresh organic blueberries
2 cups of red grapes
1 pomegranate, only the seeds

How to Make It:

To prepare the pomegranate, start by cutting the knob off the top of the fruit. Then use a very sharp knife to score the fruit, scoring in quarters. Pull away the sections of the rind. Hold the rind over cold water, popping the seeds off the rind. In the cold water, use your fingers to get the membranes off the seeds. Do this gently to avoid damaging the seeds. Simply allow the pith to go to the top of the water and remove it. Drain the seeds.

Wash the blueberries and the grapes thoroughly in a colander before you juice them, even if they are organic.

Place the pomegranate seeds in the juicer first, juicing them. Then process the blueberries and the red grapes, juicing them. Mix the juices together when complete. Pour the juice over some ice and enjoy right away.

Pumpkin Pineapple Juice Recipe

If you are making juices during the fall, you will definitely want to give this recipe a try, since pumpkins are more readily available during the fall months. Pumpkins offer excellent nutrition and they are very rich in vitamins like vitamin C and vitamin A. These vitamins can help to keep skin healthy, prevent aging and keep your immune system strong. The addition of pineapple and apples to this juice gives it a tropical flavor and the spices really give the juice a great taste.

What You'll Need:

½ cup of pineapple chunks
1 small pumpkin
2 green apples, such as granny smith
¼ teaspoon of allspice
¼ teaspoon of ginger
Purified water to taste

How to Make It:

Make sure the pumpkin is washed before you begin working with it. Then you will want cut the top off the pumpkin, scooping out the pumpkin flesh. Make sure you remove the seeds from the pumpkin flesh and do not put the pumpkin rind in the juicer.

Wash the apples and then core them to ensure all the seeds are removed. Leave the peelings on the apples.

Run the pumpkin flesh through the juicer. If you have a lot of pulp left, you can run it through the juicer again to extract more juice. Then, juice the pineapple and the apples. Mix the juices all together. Add the allspice and the ginger to the juice, mixing to combine. Add purified water to the juice until you have a flavor you enjoy. Drink the juice right away.

Body Cleansing Celery Juice Recipe

Celery is a great ingredient for cleaning out your body. It has a lot of water in it, which helps cleanse out the body. While this juice will help cleanse your body, it also contains some great nutrients from the spinach included. The beet included is a great cleansing ingredient as well. Drink this juice and enjoy getting a nice cleanse, which will help you lose weight and feel healthier. While the juice does have a very strong green taste to it, it really works so give it a try.

What You'll Need:

1 bunch of fresh cilantro
4 stalks of celery with the leaves
1 large handful of spinach
½ a beet

How to Make It:

Wash the beet and the celery stalks carefully. Cut the celery and the ½ a beet into pieces so they can be easily juiced. Place the cilantro and the spinach in a large colander, running water over them to rinse the leaves well. Allow to drain for a few minutes before you begin juicing.

Process the cilantro and the spinach through the juicer first. Last, add the celery and beet to the juicer, juicing until complete. Make sure that you mix the juices together very well to combined the flavors. Place in a glass and drink right away. If you are not fond of the flavor, try drinking it quickly while it is lukewarm to quickly get it down.

Chapter 5: Your 7 Day Juicing Diet Meal Plan

As you go on your juicing diet, you may be a bit unfamiliar with how to get started. To help you more easily begin the juicing diet, we've developed a helpful 7-day juicing diet meal plan to help you through those first days. Keep in mind, after a few days of juicing, you should go back to a regular diet. Juicing long term is usually unhealthy. However, even after you spend some time on the juicing diet, you can continue to use these recipes to replace a meal during your day as you continue to lead a healthy lifestyle. These juices are also great if your body is feeling a bit down and you want to get a large dose of great nutrients that your body needs. Begin your diet using this meal plan for great results. Feel free to mix and match days up if you want to keep things interesting and to your own unique taste.

Day 1:

Breakfast: Pineapple and Kale Detoxifying Juice Recipe

Lunch: Carrot and Cucumber Broccoli Juice Recipe

Dinner: Go Green Spinach and Cucumber Juice Recipe

Day 2:

Breakfast: Fruity Cleansing Juice Recipe

Lunch: Potassium Delight Spinach Juice Recipe

Dinner: Citrus and Cabbage Juice Recipe

Day 3:

Breakfast: Delicious Tropical Papaya and Pineapple Juice Recipe

Lunch: Iron Packed Spinach Broccoli Juice Recipe

Dinner: Green Juice with a Hint of Sweetness Recipe

Day 4:

Breakfast: Pear, Apple, Blueberry Juice Recipe

Lunch: Sweet Pineapple Watermelon Juice Recipe

Dinner: V-8 Flavored Juice Recipe

Day 5:

Breakfast: Coconut Mango Tropical Delight Juice Recipe

Lunch: Spinach and Cinnamon Metabolism Booster Juice Recipe

Dinner: Pumpkin Pineapple Juice Recipe

Day 6:

Breakfast: Blueberry and Pomegranate Fruit Juice Recipe

Lunch: Beta Carotene Deluxe Juice Recipe

Dinner: Cucumber and Tomato Immune Boosting Juice Recipe

Day 7:

Breakfast: Body Cleansing Celery Juice Recipe

Lunch: Antioxidant Mixed Berry Juice Recipe

Dinner: Citrus, Apple, Pear Juice Recipe